IMAGES OF W

MONTGOMERY'S RHINE RIVER CROSSING

OPERATION PLUNDER

RARE PHOTOGRAPHS FROM WARTIME ARCHIVES

Jon Diamond

Pen & Sword
MILITARY

First published in Great Britain in 2019 by
PEN & SWORD MILITARY
An imprint of
Pen & Sword Books Ltd
47 Church Street
Barnsley
South Yorkshire
S70 2AS

ISBN 978-1-52673-173-9

Typeset by Concept, Huddersfield, West Yorkshire, HD4 5JL.
Printed and bound in India by Replika Press Pvt. Ltd.

Pen & Sword Books Limited incorporates the imprints of Atlas, Archaeology, Aviation, Discovery, Family History, Fiction, History, Maritime, Military, Military Classics, Politics, Select, Transport, True Crime, Air World, Frontline Publishing, Leo Cooper, Remember When, Seaforth Publishing, The Praetorian Press, Wharncliffe Local History, Wharncliffe Transport, Wharncliffe True Crime and White Owl.

For a complete list of Pen & Sword titles please contact
PEN & SWORD BOOKS LIMITED
47 Church Street, Barnsley, South Yorkshire S70 2AS, England
E-mail: enquiries@pen-and-sword.co.uk
Website: www.pen-and-sword.co.uk

Contents

Acknowledgements

This archival photograph volume in the *Images of War* series is dedicated to the armed forces service members who fought, were wounded and perished during the combat in Western Europe during the final battles against the Nazi Third Reich. We ponder upon viewing these photographs about the heroic sacrifice made to maintain freedom over tyranny, lest we forget. The author is indebted to the able assistance of the archivists at both the United States Army Military History Institute (USAMHI) at the United States Army War College in Carlisle, Pennsylvania and the Still Photo Section of the National Archives and Records Administration (NARA) in College Park, Maryland. Their diligence is much appreciated as they maintain and safeguard these superb historic images for the present tome as well as for future viewers.

Abbreviations

AA – Anti-aircraft
AAA – Anti-aircraft artillery
ACP – Automatic Colt Pistol
AG – Army Group
AP – Armour-piercing
APC – Armoured personnel carrier
APDS – Armour-piercing discarding sabot
AT – Anti-tank
AVRE – Armoured Vehicles Royal Engineers
BAR – Browning automatic rifle
BL – Breech-loading
CCB – Combat Command B
CIGS – Chief of the Imperial General Staff
C-in-C – Commander-in-Chief
COS – Chief of Staff
DUKW – an amphibious truck
ETO – European Theatre of Operations
FA – Field artillery
FEC – French Expeditionary Corps
FM – Field marshal
GFM – General field marshal
GMC – Gun motor carriage
GS – General Service
HE – High-explosive
HMC – Howitzer motor carriage
HMG – Heavy machine-gun
HQ – Headquarters
IR – Infantry regiment
KOSB – King's Own Scottish Borderers
LCI – Landing craft, infantry
LCM – Landing craft, mechanised
LCVP – Landing craft, vehicle personnel
LMG – Light machine-gun
LVT – Landing vehicle tracked
LVT(A) – Landing vehicle tracked (armoured)
MG – Machine-gun

MMG – Medium machine-gun
MTO – Mediterranean Theatre of Operations
NARA – National Archives and Records Administration
OP – Observation post
PFC – Private First Class
PIAT – Projector, infantry anti-tank
PIR – Parachute Infantry Regiment
POW – Prisoners of war
RA – Royal Artillery
RAF – Royal Air Force
RAMC – Royal Army Medical Corps
RCT – Regimental combat team
RE – Royal Engineers
RM – Royal Marine
RN – Royal Navy
RTR – Royal Tank Regiment
SB – Stretcher-bearer
SHAEF – Supreme Headquarters Allied Expeditionary Force
SMG – Sub-machine-gun
SMLE – Short magazine Lee Enfield
SPA – Self-propelled artillery
SPG – Self-propelled gun
SS – *Schutzstaffel* ('protective shield')
TAC – Tactical Air Command
TAF – Tactical Air Force
TB – Tank battalion
TD – Tank destroyer
TNT – Trinitrotoluene
USAAF – United States Army Air Force
USAMHI – United States Army Military History Institute
USN – United States Navy
USNR – United States Naval Reserve

Introduction

This *Images of War* volume, *Montgomery's Rhine River Crossing*, utilises photographs, maps and narrative text in order to examine General Dwight Eisenhower's 'broad front' strategy to breach this expansive and historic defensive water barrier, a centuries-old marker of German sovereignty. It also focuses on British FM Bernard Montgomery's 21st Army Group's (AG) massive set-piece artillery, amphibious and airborne assault with Operations Plunder, Widgeon and Varsity, to cross the Rhine on 23–24 March 1945.

However, the gruesome combat that characterised breaking through the Siegfried Line defences across the Maas and Roer Rivers in Germany's northern Rhineland from 8 February to 10 March 1945, in order to approach the Rhine River, is also necessarily depicted and described in detail as a paramount part of the entire campaign. This northern Rhineland Campaign comprised separate 21st AG Operations Veritable, Grenade and Blockbuster. Montgomery's Canadian First Army and US Ninth Army offensives in the northern Rhineland were perceived by the Germans as a great threat to their industrial heartland – the Ruhr sector – and the Nazi High Command reacted by sending reserve formations from the southern Rhineland, which had been situated against the US 12th Army Group's First and Third Armies, and from the Third Reich's interior east of the Rhine River.

Combat involving Lieutenant-General Omar Bradley and Lieutenant-General Jacob Devers' 12th and 6th Army Groups, respectively, is covered as it constituted the American operations towards the middle and southern end of the Allied 'broad Allied front strategy' of advances against Hitler's Germany in the West. The geographic scope of the Allied offensive into the Rhineland and, then, onto the Rhine River itself, extended from Nijmegen on the Waal River in Holland to the Swiss border in the south. Together, these archival photographs and accompanying text recount the campaign to reach and cross the Rhine River in March 1945.

Chapter One

Strategic Prelude to the Campaign

The successful Western Allies' lodgement on the European continent across the Normandy beaches between the Orne River and the base of the Cotentin Peninsula on 6 June 1944, under the overall ground force leadership of General Bernard Montgomery (promoted to FM in September 1944), ushered in an interval of fierce combat in the Norman hedgerows for Lieutenant-General Omar Bradley's US First Army and, before the city of Caen, the regional capital of Calvados, for Montgomery's 21st AG, which was comprised of Lieutenant-General Miles Dempsey's 2nd British Army and General Henry Crerar's Canadian First Army, the latter wielding Lieutenant-General Guy Simonds' Canadian II Corps. Montgomery's forces were a conglomeration of Britons, Scots, Welshmen, Irishmen, Canadians and Poles. Free French forces were also attached to the Allied Order of Battle.

After exploiting the Normandy breakout by July's end following Operation Cobra as well as Caen's capture and then racing across France during August, the Allies were soon poised to move into Belgium and Holland and pierce the Siegfried Line defences, the latter of which protected the German border. From there, the great Rhine River boundary, a centuries-old symbol of German national sovereignty, was in reach. As September 1944 unfolded, Eisenhower and his field commanders examined competing plans to cross the Rhine and move on to Berlin.

On 4 September, the major Belgian port of Antwerp was captured by Lieutenant-General Brian Horrocks' 11th Armoured Division of British XXX Corps. Then Eisenhower (now overall Allied ground commander) gave Montgomery permission to launch his planned Anglo-American Operation Market Garden, from 17–25 September. This operation entailed an Anglo-American and 1st Independent Polish Parachute Brigade airborne attack followed by a British XXX Corps armoured thrust from Belgium into Holland. After bitter combat along a tenaciously-held enemy corridor with numerous river crossings, Montgomery's *coup de main* lodgement across the lower Rhine at Arnhem with British 1st Airborne Division and the Polish brigade's paratroopers and glidermen failed as XXX Corps was unable to effect the timely relief of their bridgehead.

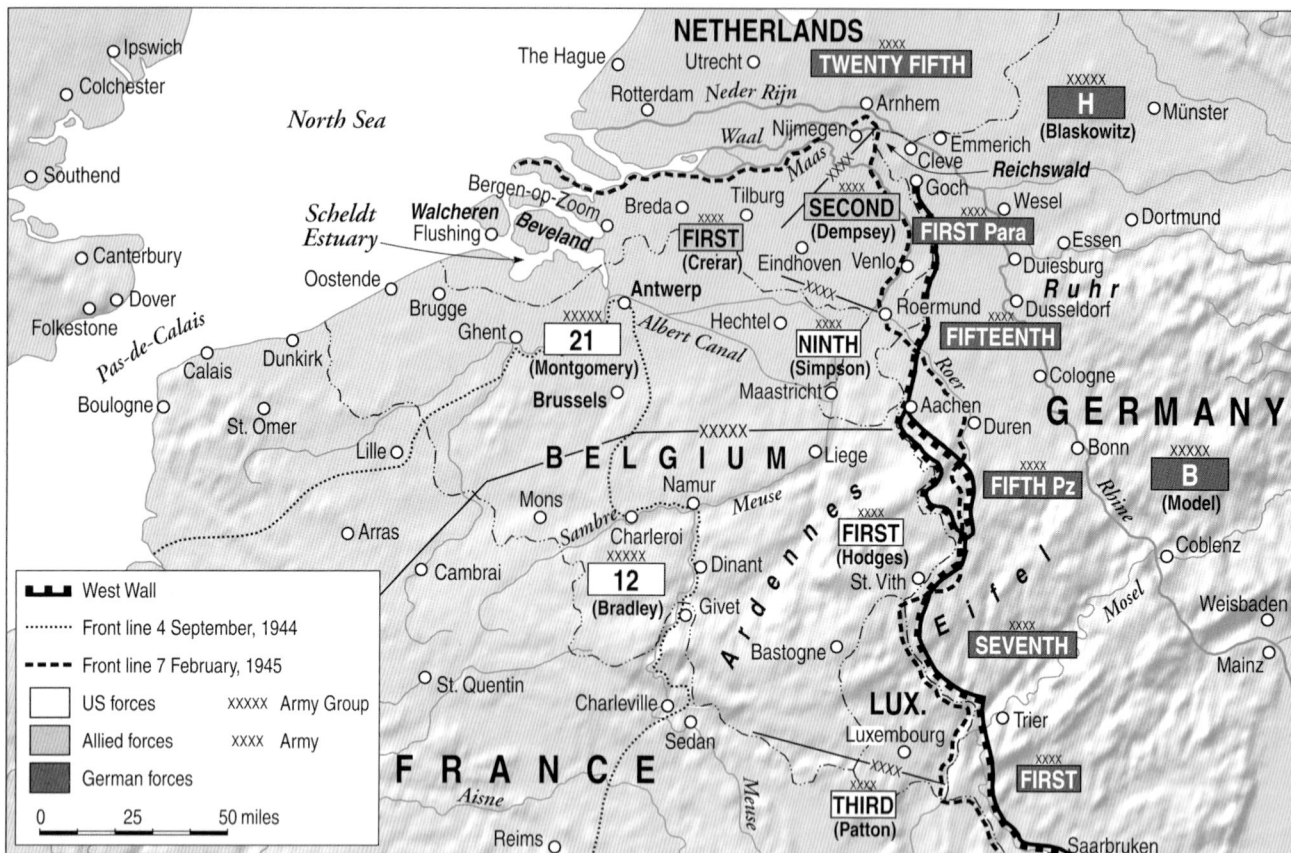

Map labels (as shown):

NETHERLANDS · TWENTY FIFTH · H (Blaskowitz) · Münster · Ipswich · Colchester · The Hague · Utrecht · Rotterdam · Neder Rijn · Arnhem · North Sea · Southend · Waal · Nijmegen · Emmerich · Cleve · Reichswald · Goch · Wesel · Dortmund · Maas · Bergen-op-Zoom · Breda · Tilburg · SECOND (Dempsey) · FIRST Para · Walcheren · Flushing · Beveland · FIRST (Crerar) · Eindhoven · Venlo · Roermund · Duisburg · Essen · Ruhr · Canterbury · Scheldt Estuary · Oostende · Ghent · 21 (Montgomery) · Albert Canal · Hechtel · NINTH (Simpson) · Roermund · FIFTEENTH · Dusseldorf · Dover · Brugge · Antwerp · Maastricht · Cologne · Folkestone · Pas-de-Calais · Calais · Dunkirk · Lille · Brussels · Aachen · Duren · GERMANY · Boulogne · St. Omer · B E L G I U M · Liege · Bonn · FIFTH Pz · B (Model) · Namur · Meuse · Rhine · Mons · Charleroi · Dinant · FIRST (Hodges) · St. Vith · Eifel · Coblenz · Arras · Cambrai · 12 (Bradley) · Givet · Bastogne · SEVENTH · Mosel · Weisbaden · Mainz · St. Quentin · Ardennes · LUX. · Luxembourg · Trier · Charleville · Sedan · FIRST · THIRD (Patton) · F R A N C E · Aisne · Meuse · Reims · Saarbruken · Sambre

Legend:
- West Wall
- Front line 4 September, 1944
- Front line 7 February, 1945
- US forces — XXXXX Army Group
- Allied forces — XXXX Army
- German forces
- 0   25   50 miles

Strategic situation. The front lines as of 4 September 1944 and 7 February 1945 are demarcated. Montgomery's Operation Market Garden attempted to cross the *Neder Rijn* at Arnhem, north-east of Antwerp, in a combined airborne-ground attack on 17 September 1944. A large component of the British 1st Airborne Division surrendered at both Arnhem and Oosterbeek on 26 September as an attempt to 'bounce the Rhine' failed. Montgomery's Anglo-Canadian forces cleared both sides of the Scheldt Estuary and reduced the fortress batteries on Walcheren Island from 22 October to 8 November. This enabled Allied convoys to sail into the port of Antwerp. Then Eisenhower implemented his 'broad front' strategy to assault the Siegfried Line along the German frontier from the northern Rhineland east of Nijmegen to the Swiss border. Several penetrations between the Maas and Roer Rivers were made by Allied units during autumn 1944 until the German Ardennes counter-attack was launched on 16 December to drive a salient between the British 21st and US 12th AGs in order to reach Belgium's Meuse River. By 16 January 1945, the Nazi counter-attack had failed and the 'bulge' created in the US First Army's lines was gradually reduced. By the end of January, Bradley's 12th AG moved eastward through the Eifel region against determined Nazi resistance. On 1 February, British Second Army's XII Corps cleared the Roermond Triangle to the Maas River. *(Meridian Mapping)*

Elsewhere, Bradley's now 12th AG, comprising the US First (under Lieutenant-General Courtney Hodges), Third (under Lieutenant-General George Patton), and Ninth (under Lieutenant-General William Simpson) Armies, was orientating its divisions towards the Franco-Belgian-Luxembourg frontier across from Germany, from Aachen in the north to Saarbrücken in the south, for future campaigning across the Siegfried Line, and then through Germany's Eifel and Saar-Palatinate regions to reach Cologne, Bonn, Koblenz, Mannheim and Mainz – all major Rhine River cities.

The 3rd Canadian Division of Crerar's Canadian First Army assaulted the Leopold Canal in Belgium on 6 October. Ten days later, Montgomery gave top priority to the clearance of the Scheldt Estuary to enable Allied shipping to reach Antwerp and, thus, end reliance on French coastal ports for supply and reinforcements. On 22 October, the 3rd Canadian Division took Breskens. On 26 October, the British 52nd (Lowland) Division landed on South Beveland Island. From 31 October to 8 November, British, Canadian and Polish troops, along with the RN, conducted amphibious and overland campaigns to liberate the Dutch island of Walcheren, with its formidable coastal batteries guarding the Scheldt Estuary. On 28 November, the initial eighteen Liberty ships reached Antwerp.

In Brussels on 18 October, Eisenhower outlined his plan for the Allied 12th and 21st AG to destroy the German forces west of the Rhine. Eisenhower then intended for his forces to cross the Rhine and implement swift mobile operations on the river's east bank to capture the Ruhr region, an important industrial area and thoroughfare to the North German Plain.

On 1 December, there were sixty-eight Allied divisions among the various armies poised on Germany's border from the Netherlands to Switzerland. However, Hitler launched his surprise offensive through the Ardennes on 16 December, creating a 'bulge' through eastern Belgium between Allied armies from Monschau in the north to Echternach on the Luxembourg border to the south. With stiffening Anglo-American resistance and shifting of US Ninth Army to Montgomery's 21st AG, the 'shoulders of the bulge' were contained. On 16 January 1945, Nazi forces were pushed back to their offensive's start line with a loss of over 100,000 German troops and destruction of extensive amounts of armour and artillery.

Montgomery's 21st AG's armies were now orientated. In northern Holland, Crerar's Canadian First Army held territory east of Nijmegen on the Waal River south of Arnhem between the Maas and Rhine Rivers. The Canadians were soon to confront a formidable sector of the Siegfried Line to the west of the German locales of Cleve, Goch and Weeze, situated north-to-south. Also, flooded terrain magnified the Canadians' difficulty campaigning in this most northern Allied sector.

Dempsey's Second British Army was situated on the Maas River. They were to breach the Siegfried Line opposite the German First Parachute Army, the latter situated in the Roermond salient between Venlo and Roermond as well as inland across the Roer River in the Rhineland.

To the Second British Army's right was the US Ninth Army, still attached to Montgomery's 21st AG. Simpson's divisions had already crossed some sectors of the Siegfried Line to the north of Aachen. However, these American forces were now stalemated to the west of the flooded Roer River.

Further south were the US 12th AG's First and Third Armies. Hodges and Patton's divisions had been heavily engaged in reducing the Germans' Ardennes salient before their campaign for the Eifel began across the Siegfried Line and German frontier. On this vector of advance, Bradley's 12th AG had its centre of gravity south of the Ruhr industrial region. For the present, the task of capturing the Ruhr sector and moving on to the north German plain was the responsibility of Montgomery's 21st AG.

Finally, south of Strasbourg, was Lieutenant-General Jacob Devers' 6th AG, comprising Lieutenant-General Alexander Patch's US Seventh Army and General Gabriel de Lattre de Tassigny's First French Army – the latter had already forced the Germans back onto the Rhine. However, combat in Alsace and at the 'Colmar Pocket' were to delay the Rhine crossing for Devers' divisions in this sector until the end of March.

At Malta, in late January to early February, Eisenhower tentatively planned to seize two bridgeheads across the Rhine – a northern one to the north of the Ruhr region between Emmerich and Wesel, and a more southern site, to the south of the Ruhr between Mainz and Karlsruhe. An attack in the north was the most rapid approach to eliminate the Ruhr's industrial capacity and to reach the north German plain, which was ideal for the numerically-superior Allied armoured deployment. A Rhine River crossing in the north between Emmerich and Wesel was limited to a corridor of only 20 miles of the river. Between Mainz and Karlsruhe, there were more sites to cross the Rhine with a larger force and, perhaps, against less German opposition.

British war planners argued that a dispersal of Allied forces at these two major Rhine crossing sectors was hazardous. Instead, they proposed a massive northern thrust which, logistically, was more proximate to Antwerp and, strategically, might enable the capture of the Nazi industrial heartland in the Ruhr region. Eisenhower agreed to an advance in the north with maximum strength. On 1 February, Bradley stopped Patton's offensive into the Moselle-Saar region and removed some of Third Army's infantry divisions to further bolster US Ninth Army in the 21st AG. However, Eisenhower wanted supporting US 12th AG advances to the Rhine in the south, which would give him the flexibility to switch the attack should 21st AG run into strong German resistance. Thus, the Supreme Allied Commander's three-phase plan was the destruction of the enemy forces west of the Rhine, the crossing of the river, and the destruction of Germany units along the eastern riverbank before a further advance deeper into the Third Reich.

(**Opposite**) A line of British and French POWs, captured at Dunkirk in June 1940, climbs up a sand-dune into captivity. Nonetheless, more than 338,000 Allied troops, with the immense help of the RN as well as civilian and merchant seamen, were rescued and reached England from the northern French beaches. As Churchill warned that 'wars are not won by evacuations', the arduous Allied campaign to permanently return to French soil and establish a 'Second Front' in northern Europe took almost four years to the day. During that interval, internecine combat across the North African littoral, on Sicily and up the Italian Peninsula from December 1940 ensued against the Axis forces with Italy surrendering in September 1943. (NARA)

(**Above**) General Dwight Eisenhower, commander of SHAEF, talks to blackened-faced paratroopers of Company E, 502nd PIR of the US 101st Airborne Division ('the Screaming Eagles') at Greenham Common Airfield in England during the evening hours before their parachute drop onto French soil was to commence on 5 June 1944. Among informal dialogue, the SHAEF commander gave his order for 'full victory – nothing less'. (*NARA*)

(**Opposite**) The Allied armada with barrage balloons aloft *en route* to the Normandy beaches during the naval assault phase (Operation Neptune) on 5 June to establish a major lodgement in north-western France between the Cotentin Peninsula and Caen (Operation Overlord). A variety of Allied deception methods (Operation Bodyguard) were employed to confuse the Nazi hierarchy of the exact intention of the campaign, which ultimately tied down many *Wehrmacht* units in the Pas de Calais, remote from the Normandy battlefields. The landing beaches were codenamed Utah, Omaha, Gold, Sword, and Juno. (*NARA*)

(**Opposite, above**) American soldiers from Company E, 16th IR, US 1st Division ('The Big Red One') leave their coastguard-manned LCVP and move through thigh-high surf toward the deadly confrontation at 'Bloody Omaha' beach (Fox Green sector), where strong German defences, manned by the *Wehrmacht's* 352nd Division, and difficult topography almost ruined the Allied plans to secure this assault zone. Enemy gunfire from the sand-dune ridge (*background*) which had to be captured for beach exiting was obscured by smoke. The 'butcher's bill' for Company E was that over 50 per cent of this infantry unit became casualties. (*NARA*)

(**Opposite, below**) Wounded soldiers from the British 3rd Division's 1st South Lancashire and 2nd Middlesex Regiments are helped out of the surf as they group at Sword beach's edge on 6 June. The rising tide reduced the area of beach, which was quickly occupied by destroyed vehicles along with dead and wounded assault troops amid tidal pools. Sword beach spanned 5 miles from Ouistreham to Saint-Aubin-sur-Mer, comprising the Allied eastern flank. The Nos 3, 4, 6 British Commandos and No. 45 RM of the 1st Special Service Brigade also made the assault against the *Wehrmacht's* 716th Infantry Division. These British troops moved onto Caen once beyond enemy-defended seaside villages. (*NARA*)

(**Above**) Reinforcements from the 3rd Canadian Infantry Division disembark LCIs (*background*) with supporting M4 medium tanks from larger amphibious transports at the Juno beach lodgement, with the assistance of sappers laying hessian matting for the armour to manoeuvre over the soft sand on 6 June. Juno spanned from the eastern end of the British beach Gold to just west of Sword. After linking all three Anglo-Canadian beaches, the Canadians were to sever the Caen-Bayeux road and seize the Carpiquet airport west of Caen. (*NARA*)

British 2nd Army casualties from Normandy's Gold and Sword beaches descend from an LST's bow ramp at an English port on 12 June. British killed and wounded from their beach assaults were approximately 1,000, while the 3rd Canadian Infantry Division lost 340 killed and 574 wounded at Juno. (NARA)

A US infantryman lying dead near a wooden log beach obstacle (*Hochpfähle* or high wooden poles also referred to as 'Rommel's asparagus') at an American assault beach on 6 June. The wooden logs were part of the GFM's Atlantic Ocean 'wall' and inland French field defences. The logs were to hinder Allied amphibious landing attempts. However, boats and armoured vehicles overcame them. (*NARA*)

GFM Gerd von Rundstedt, AG West commander, inspects a *Wehrmacht* AT gun-crew with staff officers on the English Channel coast in 1944. The German gunners are wearing camouflaged smocks and are most likely from a more elite and battle-hardened formation than many other units, comprising *Wehrmacht* 'sick battalions' or former Soviet POWs (*Hiwis* or 'voluntary assistants'). After the July plot to kill Hitler failed, von Rundstedt was relieved and replaced by FM Günther von Kluge. (*NARA*)

(**Opposite, above**) German POWs carry one of their wounded along the beachhead past watching American soldiers for evacuation and captivity in Britain. An estimated 4,000–9,000 German casualties occurred during the 6 June Allied landings. (*NARA*)

(**Opposite, below**) An American M9A1 AT rocket launcher ('bazooka') team from the US 79th Division fires their 2.36-inch 3.5lb hollow charge projectile against a German position or armoured vehicle in the dreaded Normandy hedgerows (*bocage*) near Lessay, where gains were measured in yards. This centuries-old French terrain produced American casualties that far exceeded the amphibious landings and necessitated creative methods to break through the deadlock amid the hedgerows. (*NARA*)

(**Above**) British 2nd Army's Guards Armoured Division's 1st Welsh Guards of the 32nd Guards Brigade spot German 21st and 12th SS Panzer (*Hitlerjugend*) Divisions' positions near Cagny on 19 July during Operation Goodwood, to capture ground south-east of Caen. (*NARA*)

(**Opposite, above**) A Canadian Regina Rifles' infantry section fight amid Caen's rubble on 9 July against the 25th SS-Panzergrenadier Regiment, which withdrew into the Normandy city after losing ground at this pivotal locale's western edge. (*NARA*)

(**Opposite, below**) German parachutists set-up their 8cm *Granatwerfer* 34 mortar in a concealed position amid the summer's dense Normandy vegetation, making it very difficult to spot and destroy. This mortar was known for its accuracy and rapid firing rate. *Luftwaffe* parachutists fought with unrivalled ferocity when used as infantry formations. (*NARA*)

(**Above**) Nazi SS Panzergrenadiers, in camouflage smocks, seek shelter from Allied artillery behind a stone wall during the Normandy campaign. As the Normandy combat raged, Hitler stripped units from other areas of France, the Netherlands and the Eastern Front, including four SS-Panzer Divisions with their motorised Panzergrenadiers and powerful Panzer V ('Panther') and Panzer VI ('Tiger') tanks. (*NARA*)

The colour guard of the US 28th Infantry Division leads the American portion of the Parisian victory parade down the Champs-Élysées on 29 August, days after the French capital's liberation. (*NARA*)

(**Opposite, above**) British 11th Armoured Division infantrymen cross a bridge under fire in the Antwerp area on 4 September. After capturing the Belgian port, British XXX Corps halted for nineteen days to secure the port's installations. This enabled the retreating Germans to erect fortifications to defend both shores of the Scheldt Estuary, which delayed Allied convoys the use of Antwerp. Some 90,000 troops of the *Wehrmacht's* Fifteenth Army, with more than 600 guns, were ferried across the Scheldt from Belgian and Channel coast garrisons to the Dutch islands of Walcheren and South Beveland, while the German 64th Infantry Division defended the 'Breskens Pocket' on the Scheldt's southern shore. (*NARA*)

(**Opposite, below**) Tanks of the British 11th Armoured Division with supporting infantry cross the Albert Canal in Belgium, north of Antwerp. The canal linked Antwerp and Liege as well as the Meuse River with the Scheldt Estuary. The 2nd Canadian Infantry Division had crossed the canal earlier on 8 September into Holland. Clearing the Scheldt Estuary became a priority to allow Allied convoys to reach Antwerp without the threat of German shore batteries and mines. (*NARA*)

(**Above**) British 2nd Army infantrymen dash into Venraij (or Venray) in the Limburg Province in Holland between Venlo on the east bank of the Maas River and Nijmegen on the Waal River. A large tank battle occurred here in October between elements of the British 21st Army Group and the German defenders. This area was not entirely liberated until 1945. (*NARA*)

(**Opposite, above**) A line of German machine-gunners and riflemen atop a dyke in Holland in the 'Breskens Pocket', opposite Flushing (*Vlissingen* in Dutch), a port at the southern end of Walcheren Island to the immediate north of the Scheldt Estuary, in late October. The German 64th Infantry Division defended against the 3rd Canadian Division's advance participating in Operation Switchback, which captured Breskens on 22 October. (*Author's Collection*)

(**Opposite, below**) British 52nd Lowland Division infantrymen of the KOSB regiment take cover behind a concrete wall and a bridge's steel girders as they advance on German defensive positions in Flushing (*Vlissingen*) on Walcheren Island during Operation Infatuate. The port was captured by 4 November. (*NARA*)

(**Opposite, above**) Infantrymen from the 2nd Canadian Infantry Division's Calgary Highlanders Regiment march in wet, inclement weather past a disabled German SPG on South Beveland Island on 31 October during Operation Vitality I. The Canadians then headed west towards the Walcheren-South Beveland Sloedam causeway. In all, it took nineteen days to clear both shores of the Scheldt to allow Allied shipping to reach Antwerp on 26 November. *(NARA)*

(**Opposite, below**) Members of the 1st British Airborne Division (the 'Red Devils') advanced through Oosterbeek in mid-September during Operation Market Garden. General Robert 'Roy' Urquhart's paratroopers and glidermen ran into the II SS Panzer Corps that was refitting in the area after their evacuation from France. GFM Walther Model's HQ of AG B was located a mile from the British drop-zone. *(NARA)*

(**Above**) A wounded 1st British Airborne paratrooper is carried back to the ever-shrinking perimeter at Oosterbeek during the closing days of Operation Market Garden on 26 September. Large numbers of the division surrendered after their heroic defence, while some paratroopers and glidermen were evacuated back to Allied lines. *(NARA)*

A US Third Army's 5th Division infantryman crosses railroad tracks with his .30-inch calibre Browning LMG, as his unit made a dash for the city of Metz and the Moselle River. Patton's drive on the Maginot Line's Fort Driant initially commenced on 15 September and, after almost a month of unsuccessful attacks, was called off. Ultimately, Third Army units took Fort Driant on 18 November. (NARA)

(**Opposite, above**) A line of Vickers .303-inch calibre machine-guns at the ready to provide indirect fire support for British infantry crossing over a Dutch canal between Eindhoven and Nijmegen, along 'Hell's Highway', during Operation Market Garden in September. The Allies succeeded in only crossing the Waal River at Nijmegen as the 1st British Airborne assault over the Lower Rhine at Arnhem failed. (NARA)

(**Opposite, below**) A US combat engineer battalion's MG crew is shown covering a recently completed bridge through Hitler's vaunted West Wall. Several AT 'dragon teeth' concrete obstacles are visible to the right. US Army units had reached the Siegfried Line in mid-September, with many vying for the credit as being the first formation onto German soil. On 12 September, reconnaissance units from the US 3rd Armoured Division probed the Scharnhorst Line of the West Wall near Aachen. The Nazis held their West Wall positions and pillboxes tenaciously during the initial assaults. However, on 21 October, German forces surrendered in Aachen, the first major Third Reich city captured. (NARA)

(**Above**) Two American soldiers from Company C, 36th Armoured IR, 3rd Armoured Division, in US First Army's VII Corps seek a tank's shelter from the elements in Geich near Duren to Aachen's east, on 11 December. Armoured IRs were augmented in Allied tank divisions after hard lessons were learned in North Africa and Italy. Although there were many penetrations across the German frontier, Allied intelligence failed to detect a huge German counter-offensive about to be unleashed in the Ardennes. (*NARA*)

(**Opposite, above**) British infantrymen hunt snipers in Blerick in the Dutch municipality of Venlo, on the west bank of the Maas River on the German frontier on 4 December. Most of Holland south and west of the river was cleared of Nazis by this time. (*NARA*)

(**Opposite, below**) German infantrymen race across a road with destroyed American vehicles during Hitler's Ardennes counter-offensive of 16 December that created a deep 'bulge' through US First Army's VIII Corps' unbloodied 106th Infantry Division. Two days into General von Manteuffel's Fifth Panzer Army drive, two of the 106th Division's regiments surrendered 8,000 men, comprising the largest American capitulation in the land war against the Third Reich. (*NARA*)

(**Opposite**) A pair of German Panzergrenadiers next to a disabled American half-track at the start of the Ardennes counter-offensive on 16 December. US First Army commander Hodges was misguided in believing that the German drive was simply a limited counter-attack against his units' move on the Roer River dams. US 12th AG commander Bradley likewise considered it just a spoiling attack as there was no Allied intelligence predicting the Nazi break-through. Hitler wanted his armoured forces to drive onto Antwerp, divide the Allied forces into two and defeat the British 21st AG in detail. (*NARA*)

(**Above**) German Panzergrenadiers destroy an American motorised column. The Sixth SS Panzer Army, under General Sepp Dietrich, facing US First Army was to capture the Meuse River bridges. Montgomery assumed command of the northern shoulder of the 'bulge' and charged his forces to protect Namur and the Meuse River approaches. To this end, Horrocks' XXX Corps' 43rd Wessex, 51st Highland and the 53rd Welsh Divisions were positioned on the west bank of the Meuse and in the vicinity of Namur to stop any Germans crossing the river. Montgomery also placed the British 29th and 34th Armoured Brigades along with the 6th Guards Tank Brigade Armoured Brigade at the Meuse River's perpendicular bend at Namur. (*NARA*)

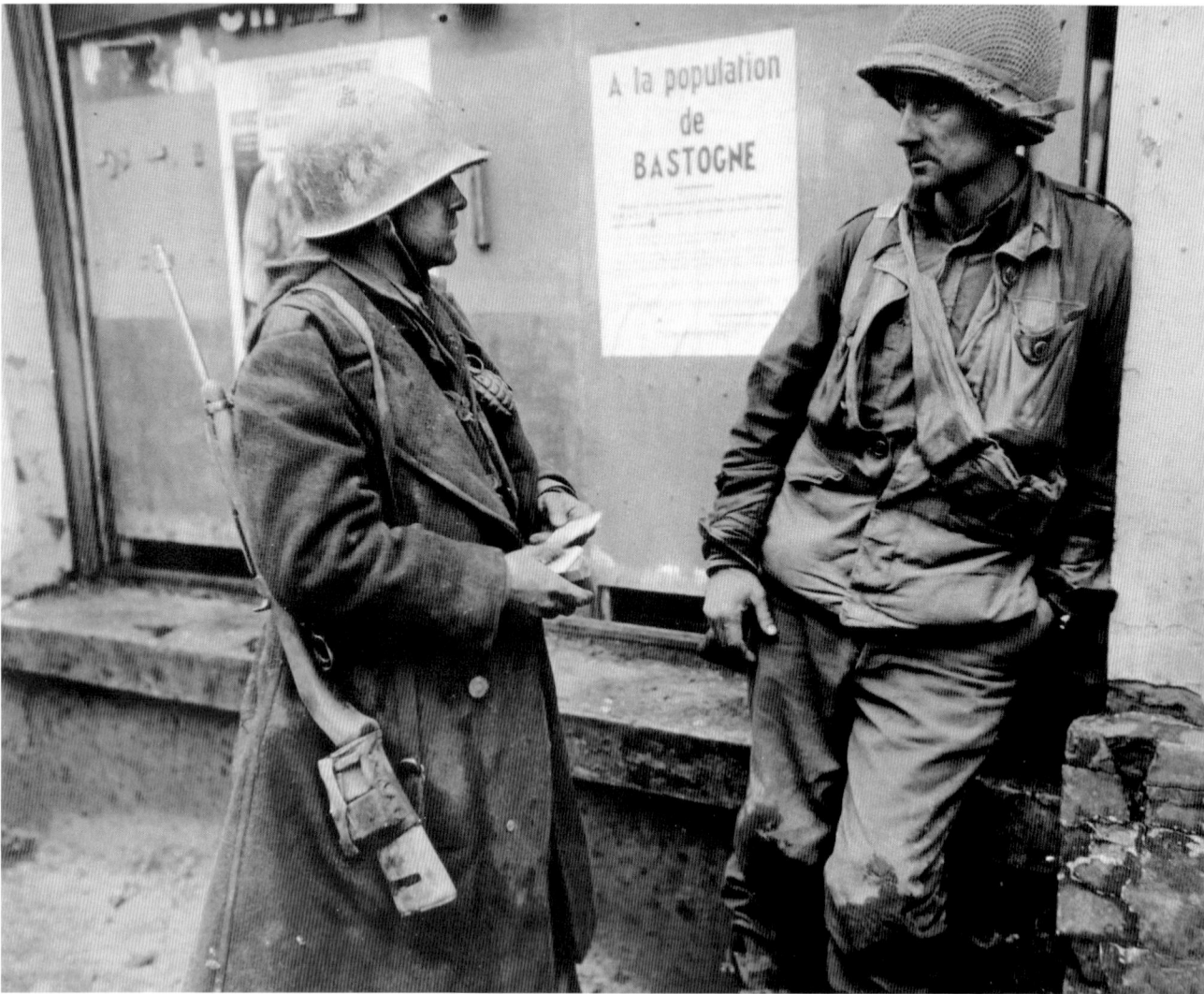

(**Above**) Two paratroopers of the US 101st Airborne Division in Bastogne, standing next to a poster in French on the wall (*background*). The paratrooper (*left*) has an M1 carbine slung over his right shoulder. Bastogne became encircled as attacking German forces believed they had insufficient strength to capture it. This gave Brigadier Anthony McAuliffe, acting 101st Airborne Division commander at Bastogne, a chance to organise his paratroopers, glidermen and tanks of the US 10th Armoured Division. On the periphery of Bastogne near Champs, the division's 502nd PIR and 327th GIR combated Nazi attempts to get into the city on 25 December. (*NARA*)

(**Opposite, above**) US combat engineers with their M9A1 AT rocket launchers ('bazookas') after having helped stave-off a German armoured thrust during the Nazi Ardennes counter-offensive along a snow-covered forest trail. An assortment of American units coalesced to mount an effective line of resistance after the destruction of the US 106th Infantry Division. (*USAMHI*)

(**Opposite, below**) A pair of soldiers from Company G, 2nd Battalion, 320th IR, 35th Division man a .30-inch calibre Browning LMG in the woods east of Bastogne as the 'bulge' was beginning to be contained during the last days of December. (*USAMHI*)

(**Above**) A British Bren LMG position guards the Maas River near Glegsternen on 10 January 1945. Montgomery ordered units of Dempsey's British 2nd Army to clear the 'Roermond Triangle', the last German salient to the west of the junction of the Maas and Roer Rivers to the south of Venlo. (*NARA*)

(**Opposite, above**) A British Vickers .303-inch calibre MG crew with their weapon at an outpost along the northern 'shoulder' of the 'bulge'. British Second Army's XXX Corps was used in a continuous east-to-west running line from Brussels to Maastricht to prevent the Nazi Fifteenth, Sixth SS-Panzer and Fifth Panzer Armies from converging on Antwerp to the north-west by getting across the Meuse River between Namur and Liege. (*NARA*)

(**Opposite, below**) British Churchill and M4 medium tanks along with units of the US Ninth Army's 102nd Infantry Division, in white snow camouflage, occupy Brachelen, an old German city 10 miles inside the frontier, on 26 January, after the Americans overran almost a hundred Nazi pillboxes along the Siegfried Line. British armour from the Dragoon Guards Armoured Regiment and other yeomanry formations worked closely with the American infantry to eliminate the German salient at the Roer-Wurm Rivers' confluence. (*NARA*)

American infantrymen from the US 2nd Division, in white snow camouflage, march behind or ride on M4 medium tanks toward Monschau inside the German frontier, situated between Aachen to the north and St Vith to the south to close the 'bulge', before Eisenhower directed the US First and Third Armies to advance into the Eifel after these formations linked up on 16 January north-east of Bastogne. The 'Battle of the Bulge' cost the US Army more than 10,000 men killed, 48,000 wounded, and a staggering 23,000 missing. The Germans lost hundreds of Panzers, which could not be replaced to defend the Allied advances to the Rhine River. (*NARA*)

Chapter Two

Terrain, Fortifications and Weapons

The Rhine River

The Rhine River is 850 miles long and forms at the confluence of two mountain waterways near the Italian-Swiss border. From its origin, the Rhine moves north to Lake Constance along the edge of Austria and Liechtenstein. The ever-widening waterway winds through Germany and Switzerland and turns sharply to the north, separating Germany's Black Forest from France's Vosges Mountains. The Rhine continues flowing northward, passing Karlsruhe, Speyer to Mannheim. There the Necker River joins the Rhine as it flows past Worms and Oppenheim towards Mainz, where it receives another tributary, the Main River.

Near Coblenz, the Rhine enters a gorge, and is joined by the Moselle River. Flowing north with 400–600-foot-tall cliffs, the Rhine passes Remagen, just north of the point where the Ahr River flows from the Eifel's mountains to the west. Here the mountains on the east side of the Rhine fall right into the water, making this hardly a worthwhile point to cross the river and exploit a new bridgehead for a drive into the heart of Germany. Further beyond the cliffs lie the Westerwald's primitive road network unsuitable for Allied armoured advances. Also, the roads on the western bank leading to the Ludendorff Railway Bridge at Remagen, were poor.

In its continued flow north, the Rhine passes through other prominent German cities including Bonn, Cologne, Düsseldorf, Duisburg, Dinslaken and Wesel.

At Wesel, the Rhine's width spans 0.25 mile with flood plains on both sides that could spread for more than a mile depending on the season and weather. Once floodwaters receded, the Germans used the lagoons, creeks and sandbars that remained for defences.

Running the entire length of western Germany, the Rhine turns north-westward to enter Holland near Emmerich. Then the river becomes the *Neder Rijn* and flows westward from Arnhem to Rotterdam and into the North Sea. Manmade canals connect the Rhine to the Danube to the east and the Rhône to the Mediterranean. Several Rhine River cities date back to the Roman conquest. Julius Caesar built a wooden bridge across the river, which served as a terrain barrier between the Roman legions and the German tribesmen for more than four centuries. The last successful crossing of this barrier during wartime was in the Napoleonic era.

In March 1945, the Rhine River was the last topographic boundary during the Allied offensive into western Germany, which contained the industrial heartland of the Ruhr and the Saar. As Atkinson noted, the US Army Corps of Engineers reported that 'at no place is the river fordable, even at low water', due to the Rhine's broad, deep and rapid current. Fixated on a Rhine River crossing, Allied river-crossing schools were started on the Loire in France after the sweep across France. Luxembourg steel mills were converting treadway bridge components from metal beams. US boatyards were mass producing lightweight steel assault boats, which carried a dozen American riflemen for river crossing. US Navy landing craft, capable of ferrying armour across the Rhine, were transported from England to the Rhineland via Antwerp. Even with this amassing of river crossing and bridging *matériel*, Allied strategists wanted to capture a Rhine River bridge intact.

As Berlin was becoming a less likely target for an Anglo-American advance across northern Europe, Allied planners focused on the Ruhr region with its vital steel and munitions industries. The Ruhr region resembles a triangle with the Rhine River being the western side, extending from Cologne for 50 miles to Duisburg downstream. The northern side of the triangle runs to the south of another Rhine tributary waterway, the Lippe River, which enters the great river just to the south of Wesel. This triangle's side extends eastward for 50 miles to Dortmund. The southern side of the Ruhr region's triangular appearance extends from the Rhine between Düsseldorf and Cologne to the south of Dortmund. The main cities in Germany's Ruhr industrial heartland are Essen, Düsseldorf and Wuppertal. After crossing the Rhine and encircling the Ruhr region's war-making capabilities, the Allied advance was to continue across the north German plain.

Where Montgomery's 21st Army Group was to cross on 23–24 March 1945, the Rhine is between 900 to 1,500 feet wide with a current less than 5 miles per hour and a depth of about 9 feet. The land on both sides is low and flat, with numerous creeks, canals and drainage ditches. The landscape possessed many towns, hamlets and farms. The Lippe River emptying into the Rhine just below Wesel served as the boundary between British Second and US Ninth Armies.

Weather and climate

If the ground temperature remained at freezing or below, the terrain was hard for an Allied armour and vehicular advance with speed. However, by the start of Operation Veritable on 8 February, the cold winter weather turned into an early spring thaw. Ground frost and snow melted, transforming dirt roads and fields into mud. Scores of RE companies re-built hundreds of miles of road using thousands of logs cut for the 'corduroy' surfacing to traverse the Reichswald Forest.

The Rhine River rose with the thaw and rain, which was compounded when German General Blaskowitz ordered the main dyke at Erkolom, 4 miles east of Nijmegen, to be destroyed. The Rhine's waters poured through the demolished dyke and submerged the Dutch polder, which the Canadian First Army was to quickly advance through at the start of Operation Veritable. British XXX Corps, an integral part of the Canadian First Army now assaulted across the flooded and muddy ground against German fortified defences and fortress towns.

Siegfried Line or West Wall

The construction of the Siegfried Line, or West Wall, began in 1938 to counter the French Maginot Line opposite the Saar region. This defensive line was a series of 3,000 mutually supporting concrete pillboxes situated behind minefields and concrete AT obstacles ('dragon's teeth'). More than 500,000 men of the Todt Organisation participated in the construction, utilising more than one-third of the Third Reich's annual cement production.

After the 'blitzkrieg' victories in France and the Low Countries in May-June 1940, work on the West Wall essentially ceased. By the autumn of 1944, Hitler decreed that attempts to strengthen the Siegfried Line be resumed. The strongest section of this German defensive line was at Aachen, which was broken through early on by the US First Army. After four years of neglect, the West Wall was not regarded as a means to stop the Allied advance. Instead, German field commanders viewed the defences as a way to delay any incursions so that the requisite time to mobilise reserves for a counter-attack could be achieved. However, by the autumn of 1944, there were no meaningful reserve formations after the disastrous Normandy campaign and Allied advances into areas of Belgium and Holland.

By 1945, in addition to manpower deficiencies, the Nazi line of defences also housed inadequate weaponry within the bunkers. Artillery within the bunkers usually consisted of the antiquated 37mm AT gun, with few pillboxes able to implement the newer, more powerful 75mm AT gun. Even with the larger calibre AT gun, thickened Allied armour often negated the effect of this ordnance. Nonetheless, the West Wall still posed an obstacle that had to be pierced by the Allies. Also, the defensive works added to the difficult terrain for armoured advance along the German frontier.

In the north, moving east of Nijmegen before the Siegfried Line or West Wall positions were reached, German outposts were situated as a double line of trenches in front of the Reichswald Forest protected by an AT ditch. The German 84th Infantry Division used dwellings and farmhouses as fortifications protected by minefields and connecting trenches for the *Wehrmacht* troops. Roadblocks, AT guns and concrete pillboxes were situated along roads emanating from Nijmegen's east towards a north-to-south outpost axis of Cleve to Geldern. The main Siegfried Line in the Canadian First Army sector began 3 miles to the rear of these German outposts.

The Siegfried Line's defences ran north-to-south through the Reichswald Forest, then along the forest's southern boundary to as far as Goch, south of Cleve. Both towns, among others, were fortified and encircled with AT ditches. Additional trench systems abounded to the west and south of Cleve, constituting the Reichswald Forest's encircling defences.

A third line of German defences, the Hochwald Layback, was 11 miles to the south on the way to Xanten, opposite Wesel, and possessed similar mile-wide continuous series defences comprising trenches, AT ditches, barbed-wire and fortified villages. Prior to Operation Veritable's start, German engineers had upgraded the West Wall's defences in the relatively open country extending to the Maas River west of Goch with new concrete pillboxes armed with MGs and AT guns.

In early March, GFM Kesselring took over as C-in-C West from GFM von Runstedt. Kesselring, as he had done in Italy, infused his energetic defensive genius to erect a narrow belt of rifle and MG fortifications at the most probable Rhine River crossing sites. German artillery and 88mm dual-purpose AT/AA guns were still a formidable threat to a Rhine River crossing. Unfortunately for Kesselring, the German soldier's morale ebbed and its former infantryman's *élan* existed only in SS Panzergrenadier and *Luftwaffe* parachute formations.

Hobart's 'Funnies'

Flail tanks were adapted from a variety of Allied tanks and were equipped with a system of chains on a revolving drum to beat the ground ahead of the tank and explode the mines, clearing a path for infantry and other armoured vehicles. Crocodiles were Churchill tanks equipped with flame-throwers, which could shoot a fiery gel at entrenchments up to 120 yards. The AVRE (Armoured Vehicles Royal Engineers) were also Churchill tanks equipped to do a variety of specialised tasks. Some carried the Petard, a short-barrelled mortar that could hurl a heavy HE charge, referred to as a 'flying dustbin', against concrete bunkers, gun emplacements, sand-bagged houses, etc. Other AVREs carried a box-girder bridge for crossing AT ditches or streams. Some AVREs carried large bundles of fascines, up to 8 feet in diameter, for dropping into ditches to create an *ersatz* 'bridge' for tanks to cross. Kangaroos were converted Canadian Ram tanks, based on the US M4 design, now used as APCs to protect assaulting Anglo-Canadian infantry. Buffaloes were American-designed and built LVTs, amphibious armoured vehicles, capable of carrying thirty troops, and a 25-pounder gun or a Bren carrier across rivers or through the floodwaters of the northern Rhineland.

German Panzers and associated weaponry

The Panzer V (Panther) and VI (Tiger) tanks easily outclassed the M4 medium, the Churchill and Cromwell tanks in a duelling situation. However, they were inevitably outnumbered. Later-designed Allied tanks, the Comet and Pershing, each with larger calibre, higher velocity turret guns, equalised the armoured combat. Along with the Panzer V and VI tanks, Nazi AT guns, notably the 88mm dual-purpose AT/AA pieces, were also used effectively to screen the German armour from Allied thrusts. The numerically superior Allied M4 medium tank squadrons absorbed the deadly German AT gunfire with lethal consequences, before coming into range with the Nazi Panzers. As the Allied tanks approached, there was always the concern for German infantry dug into the ground with their close-range, effective *Panzerfausts*.

An American minesweeping detachment from Company C, 275th Engineer Battalion attached to the US 75th Infantry Division use metal mine-detectors along a path covered by several inches of snow. The engineers cleared a route for American armour and vehicles to regain Commanster near Vielsalm, Belgium, on the Salm River on 25 January. Previously, the German 9th SS Panzer Division seized this locale along the northern shoulder of the 'bulge' during the Ardennes offensive of mid-December. *(USAMHI)*

(**Opposite, above**) Canadian infantrymen column trudge over a frozen, snow-covered path between Hetogenbosch and Geertruidenberg, Holland on 1 February 1945. For the Canadian First Army's British XXX assault on Cleve, Allied planners counted on frozen ground for their tanks and armour to move quickly. However, an early spring thaw turned the roads into a quagmire, creating traffic congestion and delays from Nijmegen eastwards. (*NARA*)

(**Opposite, below**) A British Second Army gunner in winter uniform inspects his AT gun in a frost-covered dug-in position on 25 December. The massive German armoured attack occurred through the Ardennes into Belgium and Luxemburg. Montgomery positioned British XXX Corps with the 43rd Wessex, 53rd Welsh and Guards Armoured Division along the Meuse River, from Namur in the west to Liege eastwards, to guard the approaches to Antwerp. (*NARA*)

(**Above**) A camouflaged dug-in American AT gun is loaded in the snow-covered woods along the German frontier. Both combatant sides used forest terrain and concealment for deadly ambushes of advancing enemy infantry and armour. (*NARA*)

(**Above**) Allied gunners try to extricate their C8 Morris artillery tractor ('Quad') with towed 25-pounder gun from the flooded Dutch polder. Although a sturdy vehicle with good cross-country mobility, floodwaters from Nazi-destroyed river dams and an early spring thaw created nightmares for Canadian First Army formations' advance into the northern Rhineland in early February during Operation Veritable. (*NARA*)

(**Opposite, above**) British 79th Armoured Division LVTs (Buffaloes) transport infantrymen of the 3rd Canadian Division east of Nijmegen through floodwaters after the Germans destroyed dykes on 5 February. The 3rd Canadian Division, with previous amphibious experience along the Scheldt estuary and having received the moniker 'Water Rats', floated over AT ditches, barbed-wire entanglements and minefields. The Dutch polder (low-lying tract of land surrounded by dykes) was submerged by the Rhine and Maas River waters and, by 8 February, the flat land north of the Nijmegen-to-Cleve Road became a huge lake. The flooded terrain initially hindered the capture of German-fortified villages and dykes by the Canadians, who were tasked with protecting the left flank of the 15th Scottish Division, then advancing towards Nutterden and Cleve, from a German counter-attack. However, the 'Buffalo'-borne Canadians, while incurring heavy casualties, outflanked the Siegfried Line's enemy positions north of the Wyler-Kranenburg-Nutterden-Cleve line. The German demolition of the Erkolom dyke on 6 February not only hampered the Allied advance but also cut off the German strongholds. (*NARA*)

(**Opposite, below**) RAF armourers walk across water-soaked Dutch polder carrying 20mm cannon ammunition for RAF Hawker Mk 1Bs or Typhoons wing armament. Additionally, this fighter-bomber had four 3-inch unguided air-to-surface rockets with 60-pound warheads on rail units under the wings. These rockets were devastating against enemy targets and this aircraft became a decisive weapon following the Normandy invasion. During the II Canadian Corps combat in the Hochwald Forest in the drive onto Xanten on the Rhine River in late February-early March, RAF Typhoon sorties broke up German resistance there. (*NARA*)

(**Opposite, above**) US combat engineers cross a swollen northern Rhineland stream using a treadway pontoon ferry to transport a Dodge WC62 1.5-ton 6 × 6 truck towing a 57mm AT gun. Other engineers paddled assault storm boats (*background and right*) to traverse the high water. (*NARA*)

(**Opposite, below**) US Ninth Army soldiers from the XVI Corps' 35th Division's 134th IR cross over a pre-fabricated duck-board bridge fastened to assault boats that engineers had laid across the Roer River for Operation Grenade. This corps crossed the Roer after the successful XIII, XIX, and VII (from First Army) Corps' assaults on 23 February. (*USAMHI*)

(**Above**) A 155mm Howitzer of the 113th FA Battalion attached to the XIX Corps' 30th Infantry Division is towed via a treadway bridge across the Roer River near Julich by a tracked M29 Weasel. US Ninth Army infantry division commanders gave priority to heavier bridge-building to get AT guns and artillery across the Roer to contest German counter-attacks. (*USAMHI*)

Canadian gunners move one of their heavier ordnance pieces across a Bailey Bridge in Holland. These bridges, devised by a British War Office civil servant, Donald Bailey, were steel pre-fabricated truss structures that were transported to previously demolished bridge sites in 10-foot sections. After rapid assembly with simple tools, the temporary bridge was pushed across the waterway. A wood planking road surface was added to support a maximum of 20 tons of *matériel*. (NARA)

Canadian sappers construct a section of a Bailey Bridge to be ferried on pontoon boats across a wide Dutch river to enable the Canadian First Army's movement from northern Holland across the German frontier. These smaller bridge ferries transported tanks, vehicles and troops. (NARA)

Truckloads of shallow-draft, air-tight hollow steel-fabricated pontoon boats are lined up for transport to a waterway for bridge construction during the Allied drive towards the Rhine River. The pontoons were designed to provide buoyancy in water. (*NARA*)

A US 17th Airborne Division paratrooper seeks shelter from German ground fire in an irrigation ditch after landing to the east of the Rhine River during Operation Varsity. With his right hand he holds on to a tree branch while his M1 carbine with a folding metal stock (designed for paratroops) is in his left hand. (*NARA*)

(**Opposite, above**) Canadian infantrymen march along an earthen dyke's path in Holland. Since the Middle Ages, the vital task of flood control was tackled by the monastic orders. Two-thirds of the Netherlands area was vulnerable to storm surges from the sea and rivers, especially the Rhine and Maas. River dykes (*above*) along with canals, drainage ditches and pumping stations were all flood-control measures. Intentional flooding was utilised as a military defensive tactic in the Netherlands from the late seventeenth century. During the Allied advance into the Rhineland, the Nazis also employed this tactic by destroying dykes and river dams. (*NARA*)

(**Opposite, below**) A British infantry patrol marches single-file along a rural Dutch road past a windmill, a thatch-roofed lean-to and a silo. Windmills served as pumping stations to move water from low-lying areas back into rivers beyond dykes. Often German gun positions were concealed within innocent-appearing farm outbuildings and structures. (*NARA*)

(**Above**) US engineers build a 'corduroy road' made of saplings through a German frontier forest to enable advancing armour and vehicular movement. The early spring thaw in February with ensuing mud delayed the 21st AG advance through the northern Rhineland. (*NARA*)

(**Above**) An American lieutenant in the US First Army waits for German defenders to emerge from their sunken positions after he tossed a hand grenade into one of them (*right*). These earth and wood fortifications housed German MG positions. However, heavier AT guns sunken within steel pillboxes and Panzer V (Panther) tank turrets (*Panzerturm*) were capable of halting Allied armour. (*NARA*)

(**Opposite, above**) American 'bazooka' teams take cover in roadside foxholes as other US Ninth Army 35th Division infantrymen advance onto Westerholt in late March. (*USAMHI*)

(**Opposite, below**) The Ludendorff Railroad Bridge spanned the Rhine River from Remagen to the eastern side of the river. There, a steep cliff had to be ascended by the assaulting US 9th Armoured Division of US First Army's III Corps on 7 March to enlarge the bridgehead. Steep heights emanating from the water and gorges were terrain features along the Rhine River's length. (*NARA*)

(**Above**) A Cromwell tank advances through the rubble of Udem as it supports British XXX Corps' 43rd Wessex Division, as part of the Canadian First Army's advance, south-east of the Reichswald Forest, during the final days of clearing the northern Rhineland. The German fortress towns of Udem, Cleve and Goch were destroyed by RAF aerial attack and British 21st AG artillery bombardment. (*NARA*)

(**Opposite, above**) American soldiers from the US Ninth Army's 35th Infantry Division move cautiously through the German city of Herne with rifles at the ready to fire on any Nazi sniper or hidden MG positions from the dwellings' windows and cellars after crossing the Rhine River. (*USAMHI*)

(**Opposite, below**) US Third Army soldiers move a 57mm AT gun into position along a German city's street during combat in the Saar region in early March. Prüm and Bitburg; to the west of the Kyll River, and Trier on the Saar to the south of the confluence with the Mosel River were all captured by Third Army's fast-moving corps. These moves were followed by a dash to the Rhine at Coblenz, Mainz and Oppenheim. (*NARA*)

(**Opposite, above**) An M4 medium tank of Task Force X of the US First Army's 3rd Armoured Division penetrates the Siegfried Line's 'dragon teeth' near Aachen on 13 September. The dragon teeth were 3–4 feet tall pyramidal reinforced concrete obstacles that were constructed to impede Allied armour and mechanised infantry as well as channel them into German AT gun 'killing zones'. (*NARA*)

(**Opposite, below**) US Third Army's 90th Division infantrymen pass through a destroyed portion of the Siegfried Line's dragon teeth near Habscheid in the Rhineland's Palatinate region in mid-February. Allied combat engineers and bulldozers negated the effectiveness of the dragon teeth obstacles. (*NARA*)

(**Above**) A British XXX Corps truck-mounted 40mm Bofors AA gun was stymied amid flooded Dutch polder east of Nijmegen. Floodwaters, poor roads and vehicular congestion impeded the XXX Corps advance on to Cleve during February's Operation Veritable in the northern Rhineland. (*NARA*)

(**Opposite, above**) Canadian First Army's 40mm Bofors gun batteries fire over open sights at German positions to support infantry attacking along the Nutterden-Cleve Road during early February's start of Operation Veritable. The Bofors guns often fired tracer rounds to pinpoint the enemy positions for the advancing infantry. (*NARA*)

(**Opposite, below**) A British 6-pounder (weight of projectile) AT gun towed by a Universal Carrier moves across a muddy track that traverses alternating woodland and farmland along the German frontier during Operation Clipper in mid-November. British XXX Corps, with the attached US 84th Infantry Division, attacked the Geilenkirchen salient, situated on the Wurm River, 12 miles to the north of Aachen. This successful operation cleared the Nazi defenders from south of the Maas River between Venlo to the north and Roermond to the south. (*NARA*)

(**Above**) A battery of 25-pounder cannon manned by US Ninth Army artillerymen behind an embankment preparing for a fire mission on 23 March. At 0100 hours on 24 March, 40,000 gunners of the US Ninth Army began their massive artillery bombardment of the Rhine's east bank at Walsum opposite Simpson's XVI Corps. (*NARA*)

(**Above**) British RA gunners of the 77th Duke of Lancashire's Own Yeomanry manhandle their BL 5.5-inch Mk 2 medium cannon into position. This RA piece was introduced into the British Army in May 1942 to replace the 6-inch Howitzer. At first, its range was disappointing. However, with a new HE shell that was 20lb lighter, the maximum range of this gun improved to just over 9 miles. Medium cannon batteries along the west bank of the Rhine River participated in 21st AG's massive bombardment preceding Operation Plunder on the night of 23–24 March. (*NARA*)

(**Opposite, above**) American artillerymen fire their M5 3-inch AT gun in a field gun role as German Panzer targets were becoming scarcer. This ordnance replaced the M3A1 37mm AT gun, which was antiquated in the ETO at this time. The targets were Nazi West Wall pillboxes opposing the US Third Army's advance west of Dillingen in the Saar region. (*NARA*)

(**Opposite, below**) A US Seventh Army's 969th FA Battalion's M1 155mm Howitzer crewed by African-American artillerymen clean their artillery after a fire mission along the southern end of the Allied 'broad front' advancing eastwards towards the Rhine. (*NARA*)

(**Above**) An American-manufactured M2 155mm ('Long Tom') cannon in RA service concealed under hessian camouflage as it fires against German fortifications in the northern Rhineland during Operation Veritable in early February. This 155mm cannon had a maximum range of over 25,000 yards, fired one 200lb round per minute and was utilised against concrete or steel-reinforced Nazi fortifications. (*NARA*)

(**Opposite, above**) A US M40 SPA vehicle with an M2 155mm ('Long Tom') cannon mounted on its M4 tank chassis. The gun's breech was loaded with an HE shell for firing against a fortified German village during the US Ninth Army's crossing of the Roer River on 23 February. The first production of these SPA vehicles appeared in January. Typically, the 'Long Tom' gun had an eight-wheel mount. However, this tracked vehicle more easily traversed the muddy terrain. (*NARA*)

(**Opposite, below**) US Third Army's 80th Division M4 medium tank-mounted M8 60-round, 4.5-inch barrage rocket launchers (the T34 'Calliopes') advance along a German road during Patton's drive through the Saar region to the Rhine River from Coblenz south to Mannheim during mid-March. There were two rows of eighteen rockets above and two rows of six below. Traverse and elevation were controlled by the turret. The launchers were expendable and, once fired, they could be detached and the tank used in its conventional role or re-loaded. The M8, due to inaccuracy, was replaced by the M16 spin-stabilised rocket during 1945. (*NARA*)

(**Opposite, above**) An American soldier loads M8 4.5-inch rockets into a launcher, the T27 'Xylophone,' a multiple-round device mounted on a 2.5-ton truck. There was no traversing mechanism but it could be elevated from −5° to +45°. (*NARA*)

(**Opposite, below**) Gunners load a Projector Rocket 3-inch No. 8 Mk 1 towed multiple rocket launcher ('Land Mattress') during British XXX Corps' advance onto Cleve and beyond in Operation Veritable in early February. Although the British Army deployed these relatively late in the war, this weapon provided useful service in the Rhine and Scheldt River crossings, as either sixteen- or thirty-tube launchers on a towed two-wheeled carriage (*right, foreground*). Rounds were fired at a 4-per-second rate. At river crossings, more than a thousand were launched in a six-hour interval. (*Author's Collection*)

(**Above**) Canadian soldiers operate captured German 20mm Flak 30 AA guns at their bivouac area. This trailer-mounted weapon was developed in 1934 and first deployed in the Spanish Civil War. It fired 120 rounds per minute by an experienced eight-man crew. A four-barrelled Flak 38 was introduced in 1938. (*NARA*)

(**Opposite, above**) Two American soldiers examine one of five 88mm Flak 18 or 36 AA/AT guns abandoned in Geilerwist in early March. This versatile gun was introduced by the *Wehrmacht* in 1933. It too was originally deployed in Spain in 1936. (*NARA*)

(**Opposite, below**) A US Ninth Army American soldier from the 35th Division's 134th IR inspects a captured German 128mm Flak 40 AA gun near Suer on 31 March. This weapon was introduced in 1941 and was equipped with an electric aiming device and it reloaded automatically. With a weight of almost 40,000lb, these guns when not transported on special trailers were installed in concrete revetments such as this one, where they were paradoxically vulnerable to low-flying Allied fighter-bomber attack. (*USAMHI*)

(**Above**) An American soldier examines a German five-barrel 21cm *Nebelwerfer* ('Smoke Launcher') 42 rocket launcher (the Allies' moniker, 'Screemin Meemie') in Lunebeck on 20 March. The *Wehrmacht* used a large number of artillery weapons firing rocket-propelled ammunition. These *Nebelwerfer* weapons could launch rocket-propelled projectiles from all of its five tubes within eight seconds. (*NARA*)

(**Opposite, above**) A side view of a German *Sturmtiger* assault gun of a *Sturmmörser* (mortar) company after it was disabled by US Ninth Army infantry on the east bank of the Roer River after the start of Operation Grenade. The turret of the Panzer VI (Tiger) was replaced with an armour-plated housing to accommodate the 15-inch rocket mortar. However, only a few dozen were built. *(NARA)*

(**Above**) A British soldier regards two disabled Panzer V (Panther) tanks. Due to the success of the Soviet T-34 tank against German armour on the Eastern Front, the *Wehrmacht's* ordnance department, at the end of 1942, began producing the first of 6,000 Panzer Vs, incorporating the exceptional T-34 features. The Panther combined a ballistically effective shape, manoeuvrability, thick frontal armour, and a 75mm *KwK* L/70 turret gun capable of penetrating Allied armour at a distance of two-thirds of a mile. *(NARA)*

(**Opposite, below**) A combat engineer attached to the US Ninth Army's 102nd Infantry Division watches his fellow engineers destroy Nazi Panzer V (Panther) tanks (background) in order to prevent their turrets from being converted into *Panzerturms*, in January. The American engineer *(foreground)* took cover behind one of two Panzer IV (probably *Ausf.* H model) tanks, which had an excellent KwK-40 L/48 turret gun and thickened armour. *(NARA)*

(**Opposite, above**) A German *Jagdpanther* TD after it was disabled by Canadian First Army troops in the Reichs-wald Forest during Operation Veritable in February. Armed with a 88mm Pak 43 AT gun mounted on the chassis of a Panzer V (Panther), the *Jagdpanther's* limited traverse forced this TD to be pointed in the proper direction. Situated in a correct direction, the *Jagdpanther* TD was capable of destroying any Allied tank. (*Author's Collection*)

(**Opposite, below**) British troops carry an open plywood storm boat with an Evinrude outboard motor (*fore-ground*) for the Seine River crossings in August 1944. It took thirty-six men to carry one of these unwieldy boats. Along the Rhine River at 0200 hours on 24 March, two assault battalions of the 15th Scottish Division's 44th Lowland Brigade crossed in Buffaloes from Xanten to seize Bislich, north-west of Wesel. A follow-up battalion, the 6th KOSB, crossed in storm boats (like the one above) from Xanten as did later reinforcing units of the 51st Highland Division's 154th Brigade, attacking Rees. As storm boats were much more vulnerable than LVTs, Buffaloes carried the lead assault companies for the Rhine River crossings. (*NARA*)

(**Above**) A tracked M29 Weasel, manned by Canadian troops, moves through Holland's flooded, muddy terrain. The Weasel, built by Studebaker, was originally designed for the Canadian-American First Special Service Force (SSF) for swift movement, after being parachute-dropped, across Norway's snowy terrain to attack Nazi power plants there. With the Norway mission cancelled, the M29 was implemented in other theatres, especially north-west Europe, as a command centre, ambulance and towing vehicle. The M29 was able to cross minefields as its ground pressure was too low to detonate AT mines, which were pre-set for heavier armoured vehicles. The Weasels were used extensively by the Canadian First Army to clear the Scheldt Estuary and, later, through the flooded areas north of the Nijmegen-Nutterden-Cleve Road during Operation Veritable. (*NARA*)

(**Opposite, above**) US-built DUKWs (General Motors Corporation (GMC) manufacturing code letters: D, production year; U, Utility; K, all-wheel drive; W, dual rear axles) among British 21st AG forces in woods not far from the Rhine River before Operation Plunder began on 24 March. Appearing in 1942, the DUKW was a variant of a GMC 6 × 6 truck with a buoyant boat-shaped hull. The British produced an equivalent, the Terrapin. However, due to design and operational flaws, along with more than 21,000 DUKWs produced by war's end, development and manufacturing ceased. (*NARA*)

(**Opposite, below**) Canadian First Army troops unload a Jeep from an LVT (Buffalo) of the British 79th Armoured Division. This amphibious tracked vehicle also delivered M29 Weasels and Universal Carriers, along with AT guns and smaller calibre ordnance to defend the assaulted far shores of rivers from German Panzer counter-attacks. (*NARA*)

(**Above**) An M4 amphibious medium tank with a duplex drive (DD) and collapsible water-tight fabric screen in the deployed position emerges from the water. Another variant of Major-General Percy Hobart's 79th Armoured Division ('Hobart's Funnies'), DD M4 tanks floated with buoyant rubber air tubes during amphibious operations, while powered by two rear propellers. DD tanks were slow and prone to sinking in rough waters. These DD M4 tanks were utilised during Veritable's opening phase and the Rhine River crossings on 24 March. (*NARA*)

(**Above**) A column of the 44th RTR's DD M4 amphibious tanks of the British 79th Armoured Division advances through Bislich in support of the 15th Scottish Division's Rhine River crossing. These DD tanks assaulted the river's east bank at 0815 hours on 24 March, two days before any Bailey Bridges were erected. Ashore, the DD tank's fabric screen was collapsed and the M4 was ready for conventional land use with its main 75mm turret gun and complement of 0.30-inch calibre MGs. The two rear propellers, which powered the DD tank in the water, are visible at the rear of the tank. (*NARA*)

(**Opposite, above**) American soldiers load an AT gun across the bow ramp of a USN LCVP. The LCVP was designed and built by American shipbuilder Andrew Higgins ('Higgins Boat'), with design features based on the Japanese landing barge (*Daihatsu*). The versatility of these amphibious assault craft to rapidly deploy assault units, infantry ordnance and supplies from transports to the enemy's hostile shores to maintain a landing zone at the water's edge revolutionised Allied invasions in the Mediterranean, Pacific and European theatres. (*NARA*)

(**Opposite, below**) A USN Jeep-carrying LCVP motors past the fallen Ludendorff Railroad Bridge at Remagen on its Rhine River patrol. The bridge collapsed on 17 March, ten days after US First Army units established a bridgehead on the river's east bank after Nazi demolitions failed to completely destroy it. (*NARA*)

(**Opposite, above**) A USN LCVP shoves heavy sections of a treadway pontoon bridge for subsequent vehicular traffic. The sailors manning the MGs maintained vigilance against a *Luftwaffe* strafing attack. *(NARA)*

(**Opposite, below**) Two USN sailors man their Browning 0.30-inch calibre LMGs from recessed turrets aboard an LCVP during the Rhine River crossings. The sailors aboard this assault craft were credited with downing a Focke-Wulf 190 fighter-bomber during the US Ninth Army's crossing on 24 March. *(NARA)*

(**Above**) Two US 17th Airborne Division Waco (also called Hadrian) CG-4A gliders are simultaneously towed from a French airfield by a twin-engined C-47 Skytrain (also called Dakota) transport (*left background*) at Operation Varsity's start on 24 March. Gliders detaching from their tow-lines or being prematurely cast-off by alarmed transport pilots under fire caused the troop-carrying Wacos to crash or land far from their landing zone. The slow, low-flying C-47 transports were easy targets for Nazi AA guns, with several downed aircraft. *(NARA)*

(**Above**) Waco CG-4A gliders are towed in formation by C-47 transports towards their American 194th Glider Regiment landing zone to the north-east of Wesel during Operation Varsity, approximately 40 minutes after the US 17th Airborne Division's 507th and 513th PIRs hit the ground after their parachute descent on 24 March. The wood-and-metal-constructed Waco CG-4A was box-like with high wings and covered with fabric. Each Waco carried fifteen troops to their target, the five vital Issel River bridges to the landing zone's east, as well as to rendezvous with British Commandos near Wesel. The Waco could also carry a Jeep with six glidermen or a 75mm pack Howitzer with ammunition and a five-man firing crew to be discharged from an upward-swinging hinged nose. (*NARA*)

(**Opposite, above**) A British Horsa glider, which had a greater carrying capacity than the Waco CG-4A, just received its towing start signal at an East Anglia airfield early on 24 March. More than 350 Horsa gliders were towed by American-built C-47 Dakotas, as well as RAF twin-engined Armstrong Whitworth Mk V Albemarles and four-engined Short Stirling Mk IV bombers. The Horsas, capable of carrying a Jeep with glidermen or a supply load, delivered the British 6th Air-Landing Brigade, comprising the 12th Devons to occupy Hamminkeln, the 2nd Oxford-shire and Buckinghamshire Light Infantry to capture railway bridges near Hamminkeln, and the 1st Royal Ulster Rifles to seize an intact Issel River bridge. (*NARA*)

(**Opposite, below**) A Hamilcar glider with its front hatch open to off-load a Light Tank Mk VII Tetrarch with a 2-pounder turret gun and a crew of three. Specially-designed four-engined Handley Page Halifax A. Mk VII bombers towed the giant Hamilcars. Forty-eight Hamilcar gliders carried elements of the British 6th Airborne Division during Operation Varsity across the Rhine on 24 March. (*NARA*)

A USAAF B-24 Liberator drops supplies to US XVIII Airborne Corps troops on the Rhine's eastern side during Operation Varsity on 24 March. Approximately 250 US Eight Air Force sortied for this re-supply mission. Flying at low altitudes, more than a dozen Liberators were shot down and 100 damaged by enemy flak. (NARA)

A British Barrage Balloon section deploys their aerial obstacle to deter, by the risk of collision into cables or netting, any low-flying *Luftwaffe* planes on the Allied bridgeheads across the Rhine River on 24 March. *(NARA)*

An American soldier in the 7th Engineer Battalion attached to the US Third Army prepares canisters to create a smokescreen on 3 March for the 5th Division's Kyll River crossing during Patton's Saar-Palatinate campaign. *(NARA)*

(**Above**) A British tanker walks beside his 6th Guards Tank Brigade Churchill Infantry (I) tank creating a smoke-screen on a muddy track near some woods. Many varieties of Churchill tanks, each with different purposes, were used during Operation Veritable, as well as in the Rhine River crossings. (*NARA*)

(**Opposite, above**) A Wasp was a Universal Carrier that mounted a flame-thrower. Here the Wasp is setting the undergrowth ablaze to enable Canadian First Army infantrymen to reduce German defensive positions in the Moyland Woods at the tail-end of Operation Veritable. (*NARA*)

(**Opposite, below**) A Churchill Crocodile emits a jet of flame onto an enemy position. About 800 of these specialised tanks were made and it was the main Allied flame-thrower tank in the ETO. Essentially, the Crocodile was a Mk VII Churchill with a flame-thrower replacing the hull Besa MG. The fuel tank was carried in a trailer (*far left*). The range of the flame jet was 150 yards and could be fired at one burst per second. (*NARA*)

(**Opposite, above**) A US Cavalry unit's M8 light armoured car (Greyhound) passes a destroyed German StuG SPG in Coblenz on 17 March. The M8 attributes included its firepower (a 37mm AT turret gun as well as two MGs), a low silhouette and superb cross-country manoeuvrability. (*NARA*)

(**Opposite, below**) A US M10 TD (Wolverine) dug-in as an SPA piece as there was a paucity of Panzer targets after the massive German losses during Hitler's Ardennes winter offensive. The M10 was a hybrid with an M4 chassis and an M7 3-inch gun, the latter initially developed as an AA weapon. (*NARA*)

(**Above**) A British Achilles TD, called *GLENGARRY II*, with its QF 17-pounder AT gun. This TD was a variant of the M10 but had its standard M7 3-inch gun replaced with the more powerful 17-pounder, the latter AT gun needed to combat German Panzers V (Panther) and VI (Tiger). More than 1,000 Achilles TDs were produced. (*NARA*)

(**Opposite, above**) A British Archer SPG Mk I with its QF 17-pounder AT gun is shown on the outskirts of Nutterden, between Nijmegen and Cleve, during early February's Operation Veritable. The AT gun was mounted on a Valentine tank chassis and fired from a fixed, rear-facing position over the engine compartment. The Archer's attributes included its low silhouette and rapid rearward retreat capability. (*Author's Collection*)

(**Opposite, below**) A US First Army TD crewman from the 60th Regiment's 3rd Battalion peers at enemy positions from a new M36 (Jackson) 90mm open gun mounting in late February. Approximately 400 M36s began replacing the M10 (Wolverine) TD, the latter with its near-obsolete M7 3-inch gun, during the late autumn/early winter of 1944. The 90mm gun penetrated Panzer V (Panther) and VI (Tiger) tank armour from farther ranges. (*NARA*)

(**Above**) A British Second Army Cruiser Tank Mk III Cromwell raises dust in a mid-summer Normandy field campaigning for Caen. The Cromwell replaced the Crusader cruiser tank and was armed with a 6-pounder turret gun. However, the Cromwell tanks were still under-gunned against more heavily armoured Panzer V (Panther) and VI (Tiger) tanks. (*NARA*)

(**Above**) A British Cruiser Tank, Comet I (A34), was an improvement on the Cromwell. The Comet used a new 77mm high-velocity main turret gun with an APDS round and had a lower profile than the Cromwell. Thirty-four Comets saw action at the war's end and were effective against Panzer V (Panther) at medium range and Panzer VI (Tiger) at closer distances. (*NARA*)

(**Opposite, above**) A pair of US M24 Chafee light tanks disembark over USN Unit No. 3 LCM assault crafts' bow ramps onto the east bank of the Rhine River. The newly designed Chaffee light tank possessed a 75mm main turret gun, had a crew of five and replaced the M5 light tank. It entered into combat in late 1945. (*USAMHI*)

(**Opposite, below**) An M26 (Pershing) T26E3 tank of Company A, 14th TB with its 90mm turret gun is carried across the Rhine River on 12 March by a pontoon ferry, built by the 1st Heavy Pontoon Battalion, near Remagen, after the US First Army's 9th Armoured Division captured the Ludendorff Railroad Bridge intact. The Pershing's design and armament was needed to combat the Panzer V (Panther) and VI (Tiger) tanks, which devastated M4 and M10 TD battalions during the German Ardennes offensive. (*NARA*)

Düsseldorf 70 km   1

Köln 65 km   55
Jülich 20 km

Düren 38 km

56

(**Opposite, above**) An LVT (Buffalo) emerges from the water. This amphibious tracked vehicle was armed with a 20mm 'Polsten' cannon to fire on enemy riverbank positions during a waterway's transit. The 'Polsten' gun was a less expensive and simpler Polish modification of the Swiss 20 mm Oerlikon AA gun. LVTs campaigned extensively at the Scheldt Estuary as well as during Operation Veritable and the Rhine River crossings. (*NARA*)

(**Above**) British infantrymen climb aboard a 79th Armoured Division Kangaroo for the assault on Kervenheim, 3 miles south of Udem, during February's Operation Veritable. The Kangaroo, a turretless Canadian Cruiser (Ram) tank converted into an armoured personnel carrier, was crewed by two and transported eleven fully-equipped infantrymen. The Ram also provided the design for the Sexton SPG. (*NARA*)

(**Opposite, below**) A Churchill AVRE at a German crossroads near Geilenkirchen, near the Dutch border on the Wurm River. This armoured vehicle transported REs and was armed with a Petard, a 290mm Spigot mortar that fired a 40lb warhead an effective range of 150 yards. This RE armoured vehicle's purpose was to destroy concrete bunkers and fortifications. (*NARA*)

(**Opposite, above**) A Churchill tank modified as a fascine carrier was another 'Hobart Funny' of the 79th Armoured Division. The tank carried a large bundle of wooden poles or brushwood at the front of the armoured vehicle to release into trenches and ditches, allowing other tanks to cross it. (*NARA*)

(**Above**) A Churchill 'flail' tank in Arnhem in April after the Dutch city on the Rhine River was finally captured. Another 'Hobart Funny' that served with the REs, it had a mine flail consisting of a number of heavy chains ending in fist-sized balls or flails that were attached to a rotating rotor mounted on two arms in front of the armoured vehicle. The rotation of the rotor made the flails strike the ground ahead of the tank with the force of a person or vehicle, thereby detonating buried mines. The original British 'flail' tank was a modified Matilda Infantry (I) tank, developed in North Africa in 1942 as the Scorpion. (*NARA*)

(**Opposite, below**) A column of Twoby Armoured Ramp Carrier, or ARK bridging carriers, moves along a German road. The ARK was a turretless Churchill tank that carried two folding bridges, which when unfolded spanned a 65-foot-long length of ditch or obstacle for other vehicles to cross over. (*NARA*)

(**Opposite, above**) British sappers use sniffer dogs to detect Nazi mines made of plastic and wood along the Helmond to Venlo railway line during an advance on the Dutch-Belgian border. (*NARA*)

(**Opposite, below**) Three US infantrymen man their venerable Browning M1917 0.30-inch calibre, water-cooled MMG from a prepared position to provide indirect fire support. The ammunition belt fed from a can (*left, foreground*), while a hose, at the bottom of the barrel's front, was connected to a water can. This weapon first saw service in France during the First World War. However, it was still the standard US armed forces' MMG in all Second World War theatres of combat. (*NARA*)

(**Above**) A triad of heavier defensive weaponry manned by an American combat unit amid the ruins of a recently occupied German town's street. These include an M5 3-inch AT gun, a Browning M2HB 0.5-inch calibre HMG and an M9A1 bazooka. The M5 ordnance replaced the M3A1 37mm AT gun, the latter antiquated in the ETO at this time. The tripod-mounted, air-cooled Browning HMG, typically deployed in a defensive position due to its weight of 85lb, had a cyclic firing rate of more than 500 rounds per minute. Coupled with the 0.50-inch calibre cartridge, this HMG was devastating on attacking *Wehrmacht* infantry formations and soft-skinned vehicles. The bazooka was essentially a tube that fired a 2.6-inch HE shaped-charge warhead at enemy tanks' vulnerable areas (treads and flanks) at short range. (*NARA*)

A PIAT Mk 1 weapon crew with their weapon deployed against a Nazi fortification. It could be carried and operated by one man, but was usually assigned to a two-man team. The PIAT made its combat debut during the Sicily invasion after being designed to provide an effective, inexpensive portable AT weapon for infantrymen. The weapon's design was based on the spigot mortar system that launched a 2.5lb bomb using a spring and a cartridge in the tail of the projectile. The weight of the PIAT was 32lb unloaded and had an operational range of 115 yards for direct fire against armoured vehicles and 350 yards in an indirect fire mode against bunkers or fortified houses. There was no muzzle smoke to give away the location of the crew. However, there was a powerful recoil and some difficulty in cocking the spring mechanism. (*NARA*)

Three US 17th Airborne Division paratroopers load their new M18 57mm shoulder-fired (although there were also monopod and tripods) recoilless AT gun, which could also be used in an anti-personnel method. As shown, the M18 was breech-loaded and its single shell had a lower velocity than cannon, with greater accuracy than the bazooka's unguided rocket. There was almost no recoil with the weapon. The US 507th PIR had been recently equipped with this weapon and it was put to immediate use against German Panzer VI (Tiger) tanks and Panzergrenadiers counter-attacking the paratroopers as they moved on Diersfordt Castle during Operation Varsity on 24 March. (*Author's Collection*)

Chapter Three

Commanders and Combatants

Northern Rhineland Front

For the thrust across the German frontier into the northern Rhineland, Montgomery's 21st AG rivalled the troop strength used during the Normandy campaign. General Henry Crerar's Canadian First Army's composition for February's Operation Veritable was only partially Canadian. The other major portions were the English, Scottish and Welsh divisions of Lieutenant-General Horrocks' British XXX Corps and Lieutenant-General William Simpson's US Ninth Army. For the Rhine River crossings on 23–24 March, the extent of 21st AG's supplies, river crossing vehicles and assault craft was even more formidable, typical of Montgomery's assault planning. The 21st AG deployed an overwhelming 5,500 guns of all types for the massive preparatory artillery bombardment. Tens of thousands of British, Canadian and American combat engineers assembled for the vital bridging operations after the initial Rhine River assaults to unleash the massed armoured divisions of the British Second (under the command of Lieutenant-General Miles Dempsey) and US Ninth Armies towards the Ruhr industrial region.

The Nazis were reeling after a failed Ardennes winter offensive with a staggering number of German troops killed or captured. Coupled with the Soviet juggernaut along the Eastern Front, the *Wehrmacht* formations varied considerably in strength and resorted to *Volkssturm* militia, comprising teenage boys, old men and women to resist the Allied advance into the Rhineland and eastward to the Rhine River.

Montgomery's intelligence staff estimated around 85,000 German troops opposite his 22-mile northern Rhineland front under the command of AG H General Johannes Blaskowitz. These forces comprised the Twenty-Fifth Army in Holland, under General Günther von Blumentritt, and the First Parachute Army, under General Alfred Schlemm, the latter of which covered the Rhine River 6 miles west of Emmerich south-west to Gennap on the Maas River.

Schlemm's right wing was XLVII Corps, the mobile reserve of AG H, commanded by General Heinrich Freiherr von Luttwitz, who spearheaded the Ardennes breakthrough. XLVII Corps had the 6th Parachute and the 116th and 15th Panzer Grenadier Divisions. The two Panzergrenadier formations were re-fitting after the Ardennes retreat along the northern Rhineland's major route from Nijmegen to

Wesel, the latter with its Rhine River bridges. XLVII Corps defended the sector from the Rhine River to Udem, a fortified town south-east of the Reichswald Forest.

From Udem to Weeze, the German II Parachute Corps, under General Eugen Meindl, defended this sector with his 7th and 8th Parachute Divisions, comprising fanatical *Luftwaffe* troops. In addition, Meindl commanded the 84th Infantry Division, considered a weak unit of older men and semi-invalids. General Straube's LXXXVI Infantry Corps, comprising the solid 180th and 190th Infantry Divisions, was situated from the south of Weeze to Venlo. The last sector of the northern Rhineland front from the south of Venlo to Roermond was defended by a weakened LXV Infantry Corps.

American front

Lieutenant-General Omar Bradley's US 12th AG comprised Lieutenant-Generals Courtney Hodges' First Army and George Patton's Third Army, both of which advanced through the Schnee Eifel, after the Ardennes' salient was reduced, and across the Siegfried Line into the Rhineland towards Remagen on the Rhine and the Saar-Palatinate region leading to its river crossings respectively. Further south was the US 6th AG, under Lieutenant-General Jacob Devers, comprising the Lieutenant-General Alexander Patch's US Seventh Army and General Jean de Lattre de Tassigny's First French Army.

German AG B, under GFM Walther Model, defended against the US 12th AG's advances with the *Wehrmacht's* Fifteenth and Fifth Panzer Armies from south of the Ruhr region to the vicinity of Coblenz. The Fifteenth Army, under command of General von Zangen, faced not the only infantry shortages within his sector, but also critical armour deficiencies (only 300 tanks and assault guns mustered), the 9th Panzer Division had fewer than forty tanks and assault guns, while the previously powerful Panzer *Lehr* Division had only fifty.

The German command structure at Remagen was also chaotic with different control directives emanating from Wiesbaden, Coblenz and Bonn. Finally, on 1 March, the command of Remagen's Ludendorff Railroad Bridge was relegated to German General Major Walter Botsch's command in the Bonn sector, reflecting Model's fear of an American assault on that latter Rhine city. At Remagen, a mixed command of engineer, older soldier and convalescent companies, prepared the demolitions of the railroad bridge across the Rhine River in case the US First Army approached.

General Paul Hausser's understrength AG H, comprising the Nazi Seventh and First Armies, combated the US Third and Seventh Armies in the triangular Saar-Palatinate region. Patch's Seventh Army advances in mid-March against the Siegfried Line threatened to cut off General Hans-Gustav Felber's German Seventh Army, and the *Wehrmacht's* First Army to the south was also compelled to retreat from the West Wall under GFM Albert Kesselring's direction.

A smiling SHAEF commander, Eisenhower (*background*), with his US Third Army leader, Patton (*foreground*), at the latter's HQ on 16 March. Patton, obsessed with crossing the Rhine River before Montgomery's massive set-piece Operation Plunder, prodded his XII Corps commander, Manton Eddy, to cross the river on the night of 22–23 March near Oppenheim, 15 miles south of Mainz instead of the next day. Patton's liaison officer released details of Eddy's *coup de main* Rhine River crossing with the 23rd IR at 2200 hours on 22 March without preparatory bombardment. By dawn of 23 March, six battalions of the US 5th Division were across the Rhine, exemplifying the intense rivalry between Patton and Montgomery. (*NARA*)

US 6th AG commander Devers (*left*) with US Seventh Army leader Patch descend snow-covered steps in January. The French First Army was also under US VI Corps command, which comprised the southern end of the Allied 'broad front'. (*NARA*)

(**Opposite, above**) Allied field commanders at a meeting during the battles in Normandy. From left-to-right are: Montgomery, commander of the 21st AG; Omar Bradley, head of US 12th AG (comprising the US First and Third Armies); and Miles Dempsey, in charge of the British Second Army. (*USAMHI*)

(**Opposite, below**) US Ninth Army leaders, under the direction of 21st AG commander Montgomery (*left*) since the Nazi Ardennes offensive, assemble at Julich on the east bank of the Roer River on 24 February after the successful Roer River crossings (Operation Grenade). To Montgomery's right were Major-General Raymond McLain of US XIX Corps with Ninth Army commander Simpson (*centre*) and Major-General Alvan Gillen of US XIII Corps. Ninth Army formations drove north-east to meet the First Canadian Army moving south from their Operation Veritable gains. Although Simpson wanted to quickly break through towards Neuss opposite Dusseldorf on the Rhine River, he also wanted to destroy the Nazi formations still on the west side of the river at locales such as Venlo and Roermond. (*NARA*)

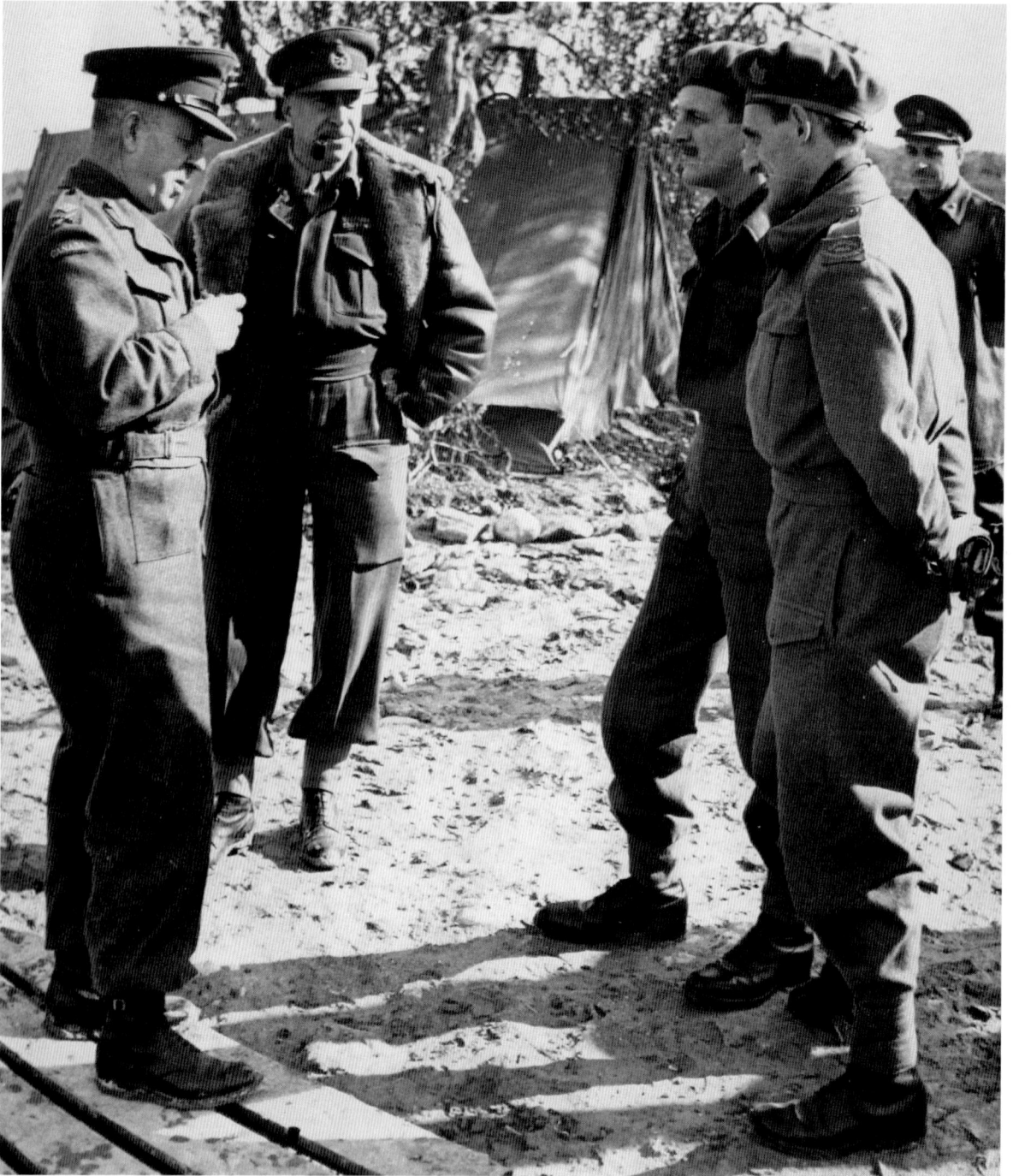

Canadian First Army commander Henry Crerar (*left, background*) casually smokes his pipe with war correspondents. Crerar, a gunner and former commander of the 2nd Canadian Division and I Canadian Corps (during the Italian campaign) led the Canadians and Polish contingents throughout the Normandy and Scheldt Estuary campaigns in the ETO. In February, the Canadian First Army, with the large British XXX Corps assigned to him, launched Operation Veritable in the northern Rhineland. (*NARA*)

Montgomery (*left*) stands next to his XXX Corps commander, Brian Horrocks, and other staff officers as they review maps on the hood of a staff car and plan the pursuit of the German First Parachute Army just after the capture of Rees and Wesel on 25 March. Horrocks detailed plans to both officers and NCOs directly, which considerably increased his combat units' morale. (*NARA*)

(**Above**) RAF Air Marshal Arthur Coningham sits in a Rhineland farmyard watching the vast Operation Varsity Allied air armada heading to the landing zones east of the Rhine River on 24 March. A First World War veteran of New Zealand's contingent at Gallipoli, Coningham later served in Britain's Royal Flying Corps. Earlier in the Second World War, he teamed with Montgomery's Eighth Army, commanding the Desert Air Force before becoming C-in-C of the 2nd Tactical Air Force in the ETO. (*NARA*)

(**Opposite, above**) Major-General Matthew Ridgway (*left*), the XVIII Airborne Corps commander, and Montgomery, decorate Brigadier James Hill, the motivating leader of the British 6th Airborne Division's 3rd Parachute Brigade after Operation Varsity. (*Author's Collection*)

(**Opposite, below**) A Canadian armoured crewman atop his tank's turret, wearing a tanker's oversuit ('pixie suit'), with his arm resting on a Bren 0.303-inch calibre LMG on an AA monopod. The pixie suit, worn by British and Commonwealth tankers during winter combat, was a heavyweight, light khaki-coloured garb with two rows of zippers covering the tanker from the throat to the ankles. (*NARA*)

(**Opposite, above**) Canadian infantrymen from the Ontario Regiment, one of Canada's oldest reserve formations, and part of the Royal Canadian Armoured Corps march through Blankenberge on the Belgian coast on the North Sea after its liberation. In August 1943, it was also designated the 11th Army Tank Regiment. This unit saw action in Sicily and on the Italian mainland as well as with the I Canadian Corps in north-west Europe. (*NARA*)

(**Above**) Canadian infantrymen hold onto each other tightly atop a Churchill Infantry (I) tank as it lurches in Dutch polder during the Scheldt Estuary campaign to open the sea-lanes to Antwerp. The 3rd Canadian Division, during Operation Switchback, captured Breskens, a city on the northern tip of the Netherlands, in late October. Then the Canadians, along with British infantry, RM and British commandos, amphibiously assaulted Walcheren and South Beveland islands. It was the first time since the failed August 1942 Dieppe raid that a fortified harbour, Flushing (*Vlissingen*), was to be seized. (*NARA*)

(**Opposite, below**) Canadian infantrymen file along to board their LVTs (Buffaloes), which served as armoured amphibious personnel carriers. LVTs were developed from Florida Everglades watercraft designs. Each LVT, crewed by REs or tank crewmen, carried thirty infantrymen or four tons of cargo, the latter including small guns or vehicles. They were armed with 20mm Polsen guns to provide some firepower when approaching Nazi-defended shores. The maximum speed was 25mph on land and 7mph in the water. (*NARA*)

(**Above**) A quartet of camouflaged Canadian snipers on the Dutch-German border. They are wearing standard British battledress and non-camouflaged Dennison airborne smocks. Their weapon is a No. 4 Mk I (T) sniper rifle with a No. 32 scope. (*NARA*)

(**Opposite, above**) Two Canadian signalmen examine a hidden German MG in a reinforced, camouflaged dugout. British and Canadian troops faced a determined Nazi foe as the frontier was crossed from Holland, with ample use of terrain features and fortified positions to delay the Allied advance. (*NARA*)

(**Opposite, below**) Canadian sappers attempt to launch a second Bailey Bridge pontoon ferry across a Dutch waterway. An M10 TD (Wolverine) is in the process of making the crossing (*background*). (*NARA*)

A private from Pennsylvania, serving as forward observer for an FA battalion in the US Third Army, peers through his periscope binoculars from within a corrugated steel dug-out concealed within tall grass on the west bank of the Saar in late November during Patton's Lorraine campaign. Patton's forces during this drive reached the West Wall to the east of the Maginot Line. *(NARA)*

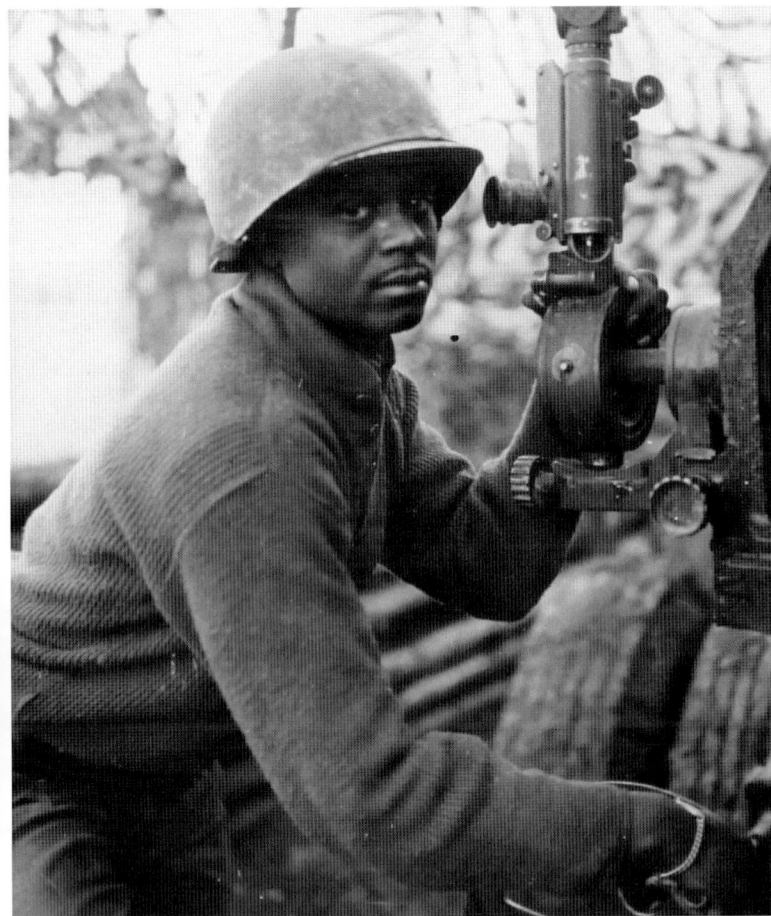

A sergeant from Mississippi, serving in an African-American FA battalion assigned to the US 90th Infantry Division, is shown manning the sight of an 8-inch Howitzer in Germany in late December. (*NARA*)

A US Ninth Army's 5th Armoured Division sergeant from Ohio watches a burning Nazi SPG (probably a StuG III *Ausf.* F) on a Panzer III chassis. The SPG was destroyed with a 'bazooka' and hand-grenades near Julich on the Roer River's east bank during Operation Grenade in late February. (*NARA*)

Two US First Army privates from Pennsylvania and Illinois in a wooded area with a 0.30-inch calibre LMG and a BAR near Paffendorf, west of Cologne on 2 March. After liberating Aachen and fierce fighting in the Huertgen Forest and for the Roer River dams, First Army units were soon to be poised along the Rhine River at Cologne, Bonn and Remagen. (NARA)

US First Army Lieutenant Karl Timmermann of III Corps' Company A, 27th Armored Infantry Battalion, 9th Armoured Division. German-born, this Nebraska resident enlisted in the US Army in 1940, although he had uncles in the *Wehrmacht*. Timmermann was the first American officer to cross the Rhine River over the Ludendorff Railway Bridge at Remagen on 7 March. (*NARA*)

US Ninth Army medics with their stretchers nearby take cover near an unassembled duck-board footbridge during an enemy mortar barrage on the west bank of the Roer River during Operation Grenade soon after the US Ninth and British Second Armies' 1,000-gun preparatory barrage ended early on 23 February. Enemy shelling as well as some low-flying, cannon-firing *Luftwaffe* sorties disrupted US combat engineers from assembling their bridges across the river. (*NARA*)

(**Above**) US combat engineers secure a pre-fabricated duck-board footbridge to assault boats to enable 84th Division infantrymen to cross the Roer River near Linnich on 23 February at the start of Operation Grenade. By nightfall, the 295th Engineer Combat Battalion erected additional footbridges as well as a floating treadway bridge to transport wheeled and tracked vehicles across the river to support the infantry on the east bank. During the early hours of 24 February, the 743rd Tank Battalion, 823rd Tank Destroyer Battalion and divisional artillery crossed the river fifteen hours ahead of schedule. (*USAMHI*)

(**Opposite, above**) Two US Ninth Army AA gunners keep a vigil for *Luftwaffe* aircraft from their dug-in quad-mounted Browning M2 0.50-inch calibre HMGs near Moers on the western side of the Rhine River on 29 March. (*NARA*)

(**Opposite, below**) A US 155mm Howitzer manned by African-American artillerymen supports the Ninth Army's advance across the Rhine River on 24 March. Simpson's XVI Corps' 30th and 79th Infantry Divisions crossed on a front from south of Wesel to Dinslaken. (*NARA*)

(**Opposite, above**) Dismounted US tank crewmen from the Third Army's 4th Armoured Division observe gunfire targeting of German artillery positions near Wonsheim, on 19 March, just prior to Patton's accelerated crossing of the Rhine River by Eddy's XII Corps' 5th Infantry Division near Oppenheim three days later. (*NARA*)

(**Above**) Members of Company B of the 270th Engineer Combat Battalion, attached to the US Seventh Army's 70th Infantry Division, complete a section of a corduroy road detour through a forested area at the southern end of the Allied 'broad front' on 11 March. (*USAMHI*)

(**Opposite, below**) US combat engineers attached to Ninth Army's 84th Division's 309th Infantry Regiment carry a single-sized steel storm boat that they paddled across the Roer River on 23 February during Operation Grenade. Each single-sized storm boat carried seven infantrymen and an engineer crew of two. (*NARA*)

A paratrooper of the US 17th Airborne Division's 507th PIR in full combat jump-gear prior to take-off. The commander of the 507th PIR, Colonel Edson Raff, eschewed martial qualities and was viewed as a tough and opinionated but cheerful leader. The 507th PIR was nicknamed 'Raff's Ruffians'. (NARA)

A dead US 17th Airborne Division paratrooper is carried away by one of his fellow jumpers. German shrapnel had laced the parachute preventing its proper deployment and the paratrooper fell to his death. (NARA)

A US Army medic tends a wounded 17th Airborne Division paratrooper. Many members of the paratroopers, if not injured by Nazi flak in mid-air, sustained traumatic fall injuries or were hit by German gunfire shortly after landing. (*NARA*)

(**Opposite, above**) Heavily-laden US 17th Airborne Division glidermen board one of their Waco gliders at a French airfield for their towed flight across the Rhine River on 23–24 March during Operation Varsity. The spools of wire and 'walkie-talkie' carried by some suggest this was a signals platoon to establish communication links on the east side of the river. (*NARA*)

(**Opposite, below**) US 17th Airborne members of the 194th Glider Infantry Regiment move from their disabled Waco gliders towards their objective, the Issel River bridges, during Operation Varsity on 24 March. (*NARA*)

An American medic tends a wounded gliderman near a wrecked Waco (*background*). Medical orderlies in both the US and British Airborne divisions incurred casualties during the landings of Operation Varsity. Members of the British 6th Airborne's 224th Parachute Field Ambulance were machine-gunned trying to aid wounded glidermen. (*NARA*)

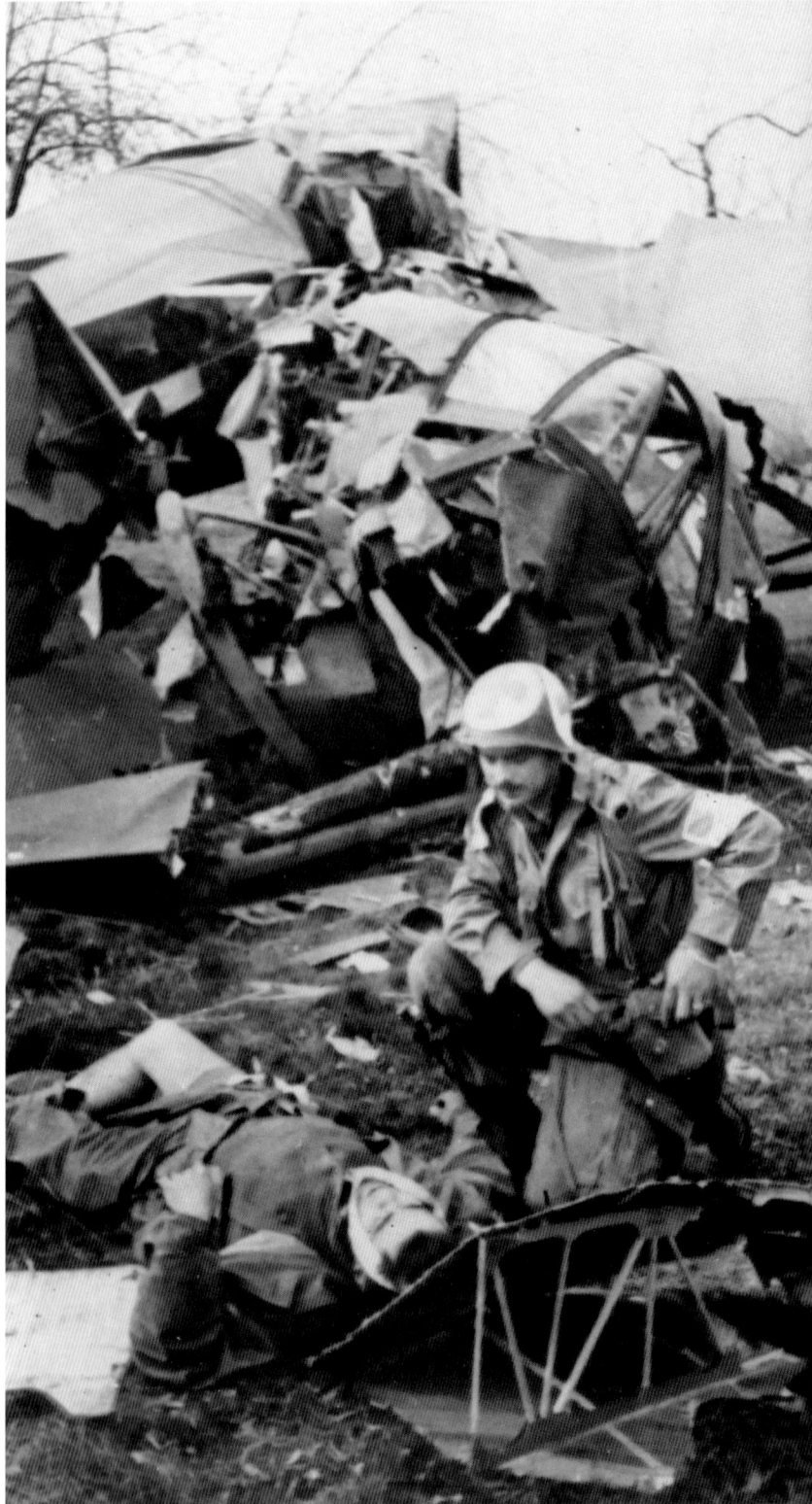

(**Opposite, above**) US Navy 'Seabees' man their LCVPs for ferrying operations. Patton had built up his own stock of assault craft since the autumn for a Third Army crossing of the Rhine River, with many Navy-crewed LCVPs having rehearsed for the event. (*NARA*)

(**Opposite, below**) A British tanker and dispatch riders listen to an American soldier in Issum. On 2 March, the US 35th Division's 135th TB captured Geldern and rendezvoused with British tankers from the 4th/7th Dragoons accompanying the 53rd Welsh Division's 158th Brigade. Later that day, the 158th Brigade was ordered to turn to the north-east and proceed towards Alpen and then the Rhine River opposite Wesel. (*NARA*)

(**Above**) British Second Army infantrymen in their trenches along the Maas River's west bank in late November. These troops were combating in the Venlo area to gain possession of the Roermond Triangle to Eindhoven's east after September's failed Operation Market Garden. (*NARA*)

(**Opposite, above**) British infantrymen in their winter trench coats advance across snow-covered ground through a destroyed German village east of the Maas River between Roermond and Geilenkirchen near the Dutch border in January. (*NARA*)

(**Opposite, below**) A British white-winter-camouflaged infantry section deploys in deep snow in the Sittard area of Holland's Limburg province on the east side of the Maas River in mid-January. An uncharacteristic winter's warming thawed the frozen terrain and turned the snowmelt into muddy tracks by early February, which impeded the Canadian First Army's Operation Veritable in the northern Rhineland along the Dutch-German border. (*NARA*)

(**Opposite, above**) A heavily kitted section of the 15th Scottish Division's 6th KOSB, as part of the British Second Army's XII Corps, advances past dead Germans along a wooded path in late March on the east side of the Rhine River. (*Author's Collection*)

(**Opposite, below**) RAMC personnel and stretcher-borne wounded British soldiers crouch in a trench as low trajectory German 88mm shells pass over them on 24 March during 21st AG's Rhine River crossings, Operation Plunder. (*NARA*)

(**Above**) A Canadian First Army motorised column, comprising British XXX Corps' 53rd Welsh Division, advances through the ruins of Goch, a ringed German fortress town, on 22 February during Operation Veritable's conclusion. The 53rd Welsh Division advanced after gruelling combat through the Reichswald Forest before paralleling the east bank of the Niers River to attack Goch with other XXX Corps formations, the 51st Highland and 15th Scottish Divisions. (*NARA*)

(**Above**) Soldiers of the 131st Infantry Brigade's 9th Durham Light Infantry, a unit in British Second Army's 7th Armoured Division (the 'Desert Rats' as shown by the jerboa desert rodent insignia on one of the infantryman's left shoulder-patch), are transported in a Kangaroo APC in late March near Stadtlohn. The Second Army began fanning out onto the Westphalian Plain, 70 miles east of the Rhine River. The Kangaroo was a turretless Canadian Ram tank (based on the US M3 medium tank design) that carried eleven soldiers and two crew members. The Ram's hull and chassis were also the basis for the Sexton 25-pounder SPG. (*NARA*)

(**Opposite, above**) British sappers on their completed Bailey Bridge, supported by pontoon boats, as an armoured column crossed a Dutch river. After assembling the pre-fabricated steel bridge sections with ordinary tools, wooden planking was laid down as a surface for vehicular traffic. (*NARA*)

(**Opposite, below**) An RE turretless M4 medium tank serves as a command APC (*foreground*) to direct a motorised column to the Rhine River for bridge-building after Operation Plunder's 24 March crossing. A variety of AVRE were utilised to bridge ditches, waterways and combat entrenched enemy fortifications with incendiary and heavy mortar bombs. (*NARA*)

(**Above**) British commandos march single-file near a Normandy city with French citizens as onlookers. Commando units were derived from both the British Army and Royal Marines. The commando unit, with a battalion-strength of approximately 500 men, was led by a lieutenant-colonel. The major subdivision of a commando unit was a company-sized troop led by a captain and his sergeant-major. A commando section was larger than the typical British Army rifle section, amounting to a platoon-sized contingent. (*NARA*)

(**Opposite, above**) The 1st Commando Brigade's No. 6 Troop amid RAF-demolished Wesel manning a pair of .303-inch calibre Vickers MGs to provide fire support for the assault on this vital road junction on 23–24 March, Operation Widgeon. A commando heavy weapons troop, comprising two officers and thirty-seven other ranks, fielded a 3-inch mortar section and a machine-gun section with three Vickers MGs. The British and RM Commandos crossed the Rhine River at 2200 hours on 23 March in storm boats and LVTs (Buffaloes). German parachute troops and infantrymen from the 180th Division resisted the commandos. At some locales within Wesel's ruins, German Panzers approached the commando positions and the British defenders called in British Second Army's XII Corps artillery to halt the Nazi tank advance. The commandos were situated to effectively hinder any German movement towards the Rhine's east bank bridgeheads. (*Author's Collection*)

(**Opposite, below**) British infantrymen of the Canadian First Army meet soldiers of the US Ninth Army. During Operations Veritable and Grenade, these Allied units linked-up near Geldern to the south of Udem and Weeze on 3 March as Horrocks' British XXX Corps troops continued their south-eastward advance from Goch. (*NARA*)

North African Goumiers from the Maghreb region atop horses, with one of the mounted soldiers (*foreground*) holding a live goat. These bellicose French First Army troops, as part of US 6th AG, earned a reputation for fearlessness in North Africa and Italy. As part of the FEC in Italy, these infantrymen were instrumental in turning the southern flank of the Gustav Line in May 1943. Tunisian and Moroccan units of the French First Army crossed the Rhine River without much logistical support in the vicinity of Strasbourg opposite Germany's Black Forest. (*Author's Collection*)

GFM Gerd von Rundstedt (*left*) with Benito Mussolini (*centre*), the Italian *Duce*, and the Nazi *Führer*, Adolf Hitler (*far right*), in 1941 after some of the Axis successes against the Soviet Union following Operation Barbarossa and British/Commonwealth forces in the Peloponnese and on Crete. In February 1945, von Rundstedt was greatly distressed by his inability to command the German armies in the west, although Hitler had promised him autonomy in the field. From his HQ near Coblenz, von Runstedt knew the West Wall would not stop the Allies following the Ardennes disaster. As for Operation Veritable, von Runstedt did not foresee the massive 21st AG attack through the Reichswald Forest in February. (*Author's Collection*)

(**Left**) The *Luftwaffe*'s GFM Albert Kesselring, who replaced von Rundstedt as C-in-C West after the Remagen debacle in early March 1945. Kesselring was a pioneering and visionary *Luftwaffe* officer who proved his tactical mettle by incorporating his *Stuka* squadrons as 'flying artillery' for the *Wehrmacht's* rapid advances in Poland, the Low Countries and France in 1939–40. After commanding Hitler's air squadrons in the MTO, Kesselring was appointed C-in-C South with his HQ near Rome in December 1941. During the Sicily campaign, Kesselring retained tactical authority over all German military units in southern Italy, even though he was a *Luftwaffe* rather than a *Wehrmacht* officer. After the Sicilian evacuation to the Italian mainland, Kesselring's strategy to fight the Allies south of Rome was at odds with Rommel, the other GFM in northern Italy. After a failed counter-attacking strategy to repel the Allied invasion at Salerno, Kesselring advocated for a tenacious defence of southern Italy by building defensive fortification belts across the peninsula's rugged mountains and rivers. Forced onto the defensive, Kesselring utilised a harsh winter climate, interior lines, and mountain redoubts as Nazi 'force multipliers' with his manpower deficiencies. He proved to be an excellent defensive strategist at both the Gustav and Gothic Lines, which delayed the Allied advance up the Italian peninsula from December 1943 to April 1945, notably at Cassino and in the Northern Apennines. In March 1945, Kesselring was tasked to organise the defence of Germany along the Rhine River. (*NARA*)

(**Centre**) GFM Walther Model, commanding general of Army Group B, which was situated in the centre of the German defensive line spanning from the North Sea to Switzerland. An ardent supporter of Hitler and his Nazi regime, Model commanded divisions and AGs on the Eastern Front prior to being sent to France to take over AG B there. Like Kesselring, he was an excellent defensive strategist as well as Panzer tactician. (*Author's Collection*)

(**Right**) General Johannes Blaskowitz, commanding general of AG H, which was situated in the Northern Rhineland. An infantryman by training, he irritated Hitler as a critic of the harsh SS tactics. He received command again only after a four-year interval following his concern about Nazi atrocities. His response to the Canadian First Army's Operation Veritable through the Reichswald Forest was initially slow. (*Author's Collection*)

(**Left**) The *Wehrmacht's* Fifteenth Army's commander General Gustav Adolf von Zangen. An infantryman and veteran of France, Italy and the Eastern Front, von Zangen was in command of the sector that included the Remagen bridgehead established by elements of the US First Army in early March. *(Author's Collection)*

(**Right**) *Luftwaffe* General Alfred Schlemm commanded the First Parachute Army for a wounded General Kurt Student in the Northern Rhineland. He was a veteran of many campaigns, which included being COS to Student during Crete's airborne invasion in 1941. At Anzio, as commander of the I Parachute Corps, he stubbornly defended his sector of the German perimeter from January to May 1944. Combating the Canadian First Army thrust through the Reichswald Forest, he was energetic and offensive-minded but, upon retreating to the west bank of the Rhine River prior to the Montgomery's 21st AG attack, he knew that strategic withdrawal was necessary. *(Author's Collection)*

(**Opposite, above left**) General Heinrich Freiherr von Luttwitz, a veteran of the Eastern Front, commanded the *Wehrmacht's* XLVII Panzer Corps from September 1944 and participated in the Siege of Bastogne during the Ardennes offensive. His corps was situated in the Northern Rhineland in Blaskowitz's AG H sector as a reserve formation in March 1945 and comprised the 15th Panzer Grenadier and 116th Panzer Divisions. *(NARA)*

(**Opposite, above centre**) *Luftwaffe* General Eugen Meindl, a veteran of Crete and Normandy, commanded the II Parachute Corps in Schlemm's First Parachute Army, which comprised the 6th, 7th, and 8th Parachute Divisions situated along the eastern bank of the Rhine River to contest the British Second Army's crossings on 24 March. *(Author's Collection)*

(**Opposite, above right**) *Wehrmacht* General Erich Straub, who commanded the LXXXVI Corps in Schlemm's First Parachute Army, had fought the Allies in the Huertgen Forest in November 1944. His forces, including the 84th Infantry Division, were situated to defend the eastern bank of the Rhine. Previously, he commanded an *ad hoc* mixture of mostly non-frontline units which, not surprisingly, fared poorly against the Allied push through the West Wall defences. *(Author's Collection)*

German Panzergrenadiers move through a destroyed village on the Dutch-German frontier just prior to the start of Operation Veritable in February. The *élan* of these units, along with *Luftwaffe*'s parachute formations, was unwavering as they held their defensive positions and often made local counter-attacks. (*Author's Collection*)

(**Opposite, above**) During Operation Varsity, a German Sd.Kfz. 231 half-track tried to block a road against paratroopers of the US 17th Airborne Division. The enemy half-track was destroyed by the paratroopers' bazookas on 24 March. Along with this German vehicle, thirteen Panzers were also destroyed with bazookas. (*NARA*)

(**Above**) A German infantryman following his capture in Vorst by American troops after he had been hiding in a cellar for several days. Many German formations comprised older, non-frontline troops, who often had non-lethal maladies and were nicknamed 'stomach battalions'. (*NARA*)

(**Opposite, below**) German POWs after the Allied Rhine River crossings after being ferried to the west bank of the river for internment by an LCM. Some older men are seen accompanying Hitler Youth (*Hitlerjugend*). (*NARA*)

Captured German troops sit despondently with hands on heads near a destroyed farm in the Allied airborne drop-zone on the east bank of the Rhine River soon after Operation Varsity commenced on 24 March. A solitary American paratrooper sits atop a farm cart guarding the group of POWs. *(NARA)*

Chapter Four

Clearing the Rhineland (February–March 1945)

Montgomery's 21st Army Group's Operation Veritable

With the failure to cross the *Neder Rijn* at Arnhem in mid-September 1944, Montgomery planned for 21st AG's offensive to clear the northern Rhineland in order to reach the Rhine River for subsequent crossings. Operation Veritable, on 8 February 1945, was the biggest Allied offensive since Normandy, with an enormous massing of troops, armour and artillery in the woods east of Nijmegen. With eventually well over 100,000 Allied troops and more than 500 tanks, Veritable evolved into a characteristic Montgomery operation. Crerar's Canadian First Army, initially comprised of two Canadian and five British divisions, was concentrated on a narrow 5-mile-wide front of ground from Nijmegen to Udem, between the Maas and Rhine Rivers, dominated by the Reichswald Forest. The Canadian First Army was to confront the waiting Nazis behind their Siegfried Line's fortified positions. The terrain, now intentionally flooded by the German demolition of dykes and muddied by a thawing of frozen ground, also consisted of poor roads and dense woods, all of which impeded the numerically-superior Allied armour's mobility.

The Canadian First Army, after clearing the Reichswald Forest and capturing Cleve, was to secure the area running from Gennap on the Maas River through Asperden south of the Niers River to Goch, a ringed fortress-city directly south of Cleve through which the latter river flows. This sector was defended by German General Fiebig's depleted 84th Infantry Division with HQ in Cleve. General Schlemm, commanding the German First Parachute Army from Emmerich, moved his 7th Parachute Division from the area opposite the British Second Army north to Geldern in an attempt to strengthen the Reichswald Forest area. Schlemm also persuaded his superior, AG H commander Blaskowitz, to reposition units from General Blumentritt's Twenty-Fifth Army in Holland. Blaskowitz's intelligence sources mistakenly suspected that the British Second and American Ninth Armies would storm the Maas and Roer Rivers farther south and concluded that there were no attacking Allied forces (British XXX Corps) concentrating on an offensive from the Nijmegen area, where Horrocks' forces were secretly amassed. The C-in-C West, von Rundstedt,

NETH.

TWENTY FIFTH

Arnhem

Doetinchem

Münster

H
(Blaskowitz)

	US forces
	Allied forces
	German forces
xxxxx	Army Group
xxxx	Army
→	21st Army Group attacks of Feb 8 to Mar 13
→	US 12th Army Group attacks of Feb 23 to Mar 10
⇢	US 3rd and 7th Armies attacks of Mar 13 to Mar 25
⊏⊐	West Wall
----	Front line, 8 February 1945

Nijmegen

Emmerich
Cleve   Rees
Reichswald
Udem
Wesel
Lippe

Can. FIRST
(Crerar)

Goch
Weeze   Xanten
Geldern

Rheinberg

Dortmund

Br. SECOND
(Dempsey)

Venlo

FIRST
Para

Essen
Duisburg   Ruhr
Hagen

Neheim

21
(Montgomery)

Maas

Niers

Dusseldorf

Wuppertal
Solingen

Roermond

Erft

GERMANY

NINTH
(Simpson)

Roer

Maastricht

Alsdorf
Aachen

Duren
Huertgen
Roer Forest
Dams

Cologne

Lahn

Bonn

B
(Model)

Liége

Eupen

FIRST
(Hodges)

FIFTEENTH

Remagen

Rhine

Wetzlar

BELGIUM

St. Vith

FIFTH Pz

Mayen

Coblenz

Limburg

Friedberg

12
(Bradley)

Prum

SEVENTH

Frankfurt

Bastogne

Kyll

Wiesbaden

Main

Offenbach

THIRD
(Patton)

Bitburg

Traben

Mainz

Darmstadt

Arlon

LUX.

Moselle

Oppenheim

Luxembourg

Trier

Idar-Oberstein

Worms

Weinheim

Merzig

Mannheim

FRANCE

FIRST Kaisarslauten

Ludwigshafen

Heidelberg

Verdun

Metz

Saarbrücken

G
(Hausser)

Nancy

SEVENTH
(Patch)

Saar

Rhine

Karlsruhe

Ettlingen

6
(Devers)

Rastatt

Sarrebourg

Baden Baden

0   50 miles

Fr. FIRST Strasbourg
(de Lattre)

also moved German reinforcements to the north near Goch from the Cologne sector. The German defenders had their symbolic Rhine River to their backs and formidable SPA in prepared ambush positions to confront the massive Allied armoured units.

The Canadian First Army was reinforced with British Second Army's XXX Corps and the 15th Scottish Division from XII Corps. XXX Corps was to seize the high ground at Nutterden, the northernmost point of the Siegfried Line that controlled the western approaches to Cleve. Horrocks feared that if the enemy defences were not quickly overwhelmed then German reserves would be rushed to the Materborn Gap, a natural terrain bottleneck situated at the northern end of the Reichswald Forest to Nutterden's south-east and Cleve's south-west.

The Canadian First Army's attack forces included the 15th Scottish, the 51st Highland and the 53rd Welsh Divisions, accompanied by the 6th Guards Tank and 34th Armoured Brigades from British XXX Corps. The Canadian 3rd Division added support to the initial attack, transported through the flooded areas in Buffaloes, to outflank the Siegfried Line to the north of a line Wyler-Kranenburg-Nutterden. The 15th Scottish Division, supported by the 6th Guards Tank Brigade's assortment of tanks, including many Churchill Infantry tank specialised variants ('Hobart's Funnies'), such as mine-exploding Flails and fire-spitting Crocodiles, was transported in

---

The Rhineland campaign and advances to the Rhine River. The Allied front line on 8 February and the German West Wall defences stretching from Cleve in the north to Strasbourg in the south are shown. The Allied 21st, 12th and 6th AGs attacked to seize the Rhineland and Saar-Palatinate regions in order to reach the Rhine River. German AGs H, B and G were ordered to mount a tenacious defence on the western side of the Rhine. On 8 February, Canadian First Army launched its massive Operation Veritable eastward from Nijmegen through the flooded areas near the Reichswald Forest and the German fortress town of Cleve. After incurring high casualties, British XXX Corps' armoured and infantry formations moved south-south-eastwards onto other ringed German fortress towns at Goch and Weeze in the northern Rhineland, crossing the Niers River. After waiting for the flooded Roer River's waters to recede, US Ninth Army (attached to British 21st AG) launched Operation Grenade on 23 February. Elements of the Canadian First Army met the US Ninth Army, driving north from their Roer River crossings at Geldern, while II Canadian Corps moved along the Rhine's western side south-east of Cleve to capture Calcar. The British Second Army cleared the area between the Maas and Roer Rivers in the vicinity of Venlo Then, the 21st AG's formations converged on Xanten, the 'Gateway to the Rhine'. On 10 March, the Wesel Railway Bridge was destroyed by the retreating German First Parachute Army.

The US 12th AG's First Army, after the bloody Huertgen Forest and Roer River Dams battles, moved through the area between the Roer and Rhine Rivers to reach Cologne and Bonn. The Ludendorff Railway Bridge at Remagen was captured intact by US III Corps' 9th Armoured Division. Bradley's other army, the Third Army (under Patton), crossed the Kyll and Moselle Rivers and then, during the lightning Saar-Palatinate campaign, reached the Rhine River at a number of locales, notably Oppenheim on 21 March. Devers' US 6th AG, comprising the US Seventh and French First Armies, crossed the Saar River and the Siegfried Line defences, arriving at the Rhine River opposite from Karlsruhe on 25 March. (*Meridian Mapping*)

Kangaroo APCs to seize the vital ground at Nutterden, and then onto Cleve. This latter fortress town had to be captured early to mitigate German reinforcements from passing through this locale to reach the Materborn Gap. The 53rd Welsh Division moved along the 15th Scottish Division's southern flank. Nazi counterattacks were feared to emerge from the Reichswald Forest as good roads traversed it from Goch, where von Rundstedt had dispatched reinforcements, northwards to Cleve. The 51st Highland Division covered the Welsh Division's right flank along the southern end of the Reichswald Forest. The Highlanders were charged with clearing the roads southwards from Nijmegen towards the Maas River. On 7 February, RAF heavy bombers sortied, along with 21st AG's 1,000 artillery pieces, to raze Cleve and Goch as well as the fortress towns of Calcar, Udem and Weeze.

The Canadian First Army's goal was to hem-in and defeat the German forces within the Reichswald Forest and then drive south to take the German towns of Goch, Udem and Weeze, as well as move eastwards onto Calcar to be in position to seize a Rhine River bridge at Xanten opposite Wesel. Further to the south, Geldern was to serve as a rendezvous site for the Canadian First, the British Second and the US Ninth Armies, after the Americans successfully crossed the Roer River to the south. The British Second Army maintained a static role of holding the Maas River line and prepared for the upcoming Rhine River crossings.

Following the preparatory Allied air-raids and artillery barrage, Schlemm deployed his German First Parachute Army's 6th and 7th Parachute Divisions to Cleve and Goch. Blaskowitz still believed that Dempsey's British Second Army would strike with his forces across the Maas River. Thus, German AG H's southern front units were not similarly rushed towards the Reichswald Forest.

By the evening of 8 February, the vital Nijmegen-Cleve road was cut by the Canadian 2nd Division at Wyler and the fortified town of Kranenburg was reached. The German 84th Division, which held strong positions over 4 miles in front of the Siegfried Line, was decimated by nightfall of 8 February, with more than 3,000 German casualties. As reinforcements from the 6th and 7th German Parachute Divisions arrived, German resistance became a more tenacious defence in the Reichswald Forest, as concealed enemy SPAs took a toll on the British 51st and 53rd Divisions' infantry and supporting armour. British tanks reached Nutterden, but vehicle congestion and mud began to delay XXX Corps' advance. Although the initial Siegfried Line defences were pierced at every site, which confirmed German field commanders' concern that the effectiveness of the West Wall was illusory, adverse terrain and logistical conditions now stalled Veritable.

The battle for the Reichswald Forest became fiercer and more complex rather than Horrocks' anticipated rapid XXX Corps thrust to capture of Cleve. If XXX Corps infantry and armour did not get onto the plains beyond Cleve, the offensive could bog down in the mired terrain with the Allies counter-attacked on the narrow congested front between the Maas and Rhine Rivers. Horrocks committed his 43rd Wessex Division to break the logjam to complete Cleve's capture, as the enemy used the town's bomb craters effectively as new defensive positions that completely blocked the British XXX infantry-armour advance, as had occurred during other Allied urban campaigns in Italy and France at Ortona, Cassino and Caen.

Also, von Luttwitz's XLVII Panzer Corps, with some Panzer V (Panther), VI (Tiger) tanks, and *Jagdpanther* SPAs, attempted to reclaim Cleve before the Allied advance consolidated, thereby further delaying British XXX Corps' offensive. The Nazi corps commander's goal was to seize the Materborn Gap bottleneck between Cleve and the Reichswald Forest's northern edge. However, to von Luttwitz's chagrin, some areas of Cleve had already fallen to the Allies and elements of British XXX Corps moved south towards cutting the Cleve-to-Goch Road. Nonetheless, von Luttwitz deployed his armoured force, the 116th Panzer and the 15th Panzer Grenadier Divisions, to block British XXX Corps' advance south-eastwards to Calcar and from there the Rhine River. Sensing this threat, von Rundstedt shifted the 346th Infantry Division towards Cleve as the US Ninth Army's eleven divisions (totalling 300,000 troops, 2,000 guns and 1,400 tanks) were halted by the Roer River's floodwaters following the intentional demolition of the Roer River dams.

Montgomery's strategy was to draw Nazi formations towards the British XXX Corps, thereby enabling the US Ninth Army to cross the Roer River with greater ease and envelop the Germans from the south once the floodwaters receded. However, the US Ninth Army's crossing of the Roer River (Operation Grenade) was to be delayed a fortnight until 23 February. On 10 February, Horrocks countered by deploying elements of the 53rd Welsh Division, which had been moving along the eastern edge of the Reichswald Forest, to the smaller Cleve Forest, situated between Cleve and Goch, to confront the German reinforcements.

The decisive combat for the Reichswald Forest and Cleve began on 11–12 February. The15th Scottish Division's KOSB, with the 2nd Gordons and the Agylls and Sutherland Highlanders, assisted by Scots Guards' tanks, left the vehicular logjam and attacked towards the bomb-ravaged city, which compelled some German units to retreat eastwards. The 53rd Welsh Division advanced through the north-east corner of the Reichswald Forest, in which they had been fighting for the previous five days. While approaching the roads emanating from Cleve towards Asperden and Goch, the 115th and 104th Panzer Grenadiers met the Welshmen and initially halted their advance. However, the Welshmen destroyed several Nazi 88mm guns, Panzer IV tanks, and some *Jagdpanthers*, which sent the Germans fleeing. By the end of 12 February, von Luttwitz's mission to relieve Cleve ended in failure due to the tenacity of British XXX Corps' 43rd Wessex and 53rd Welsh Divisions clearing the Reichswald Forest.

Elsewhere, on 11–12 February, the 51st Highland Division took Hekkens as elements of this division crossed the Niers River during darkness, first in assault boats and then they were reinforced by Buffaloes ferrying additional units, Universal Carriers and AT guns. Gennap was the Highlanders' next target and from there the division moved eastward, skirting the southern aspect of the Reichswald Forest to attack Goch, a ringed fortress town that von Luttwitz's units retreated southwards into to defend as the Nazis' last bastion before British XXX Corps moved eastwards to the Rhine River. To protect the Highlanders' open right flank, Montgomery sent in his reserve divisions from the British Second Army, the 52nd Lowland and 11th Armoured Divisions. The two formations deployed in the open terrain on the east bank of the Maas River. Also, the Canadian 3rd Division arrived on the west bank of the Spoy Canal, which ran through Cleve on a north-south vector, and advanced into northern Cleve to threaten communication with the German rear.

The British XXX Corps' next advance was onto Goch with its secondary Siegfried Line fortifications. By late 13 February, a strong German force of Panzers, SPAs and mortars was situated across the advance routes of the British 43rd Wessex and 15th Scottish Divisions moving southwards from Cleve. Schlemm ordered von Luttwitz to defend Goch at all costs. Other *ad hoc* German defence positions were also established, along a line south-east of the Cleve Forest between Calcar and Udem, as well as south of Goch to prevent the 51st Highland Division from moving southwards around the town and then driving eastwards for the Rhine River. The Germans had already been driven back almost 30 miles during the five days since the start of Operation Veritable.

On the night of 13–14 February, elements of the 51st Highland Division again crossed the Niers River in Buffaloes south of Hekkens, as the bridge was demolished. The 52nd Lowland Division, paralleling the Maas River, protected the 51st's right flank. The 51st Highland, 15th Scottish, 53rd Welsh and 43rd Wessex were all converging on Goch as Crerar, on 14 February, decided to assemble a two-corps front that expanded to 14 miles. After capturing Goch, XXX Corps, situated on the right side of the Canadian First Army front, drove south-west paralleling the Maas River to Venlo to eventually link-up with Simpson's US Ninth Army once it crossed a receding Roer River. The Canadian First Army's left side comprised Lieutenant-General Guy Simonds' II Canadian Corps, which was tasked with taking the Moyland Wood and then capturing Calcar. The II Canadian Corps, reinforced with elements of the 15th Scottish, the 43rd Wessex (on loan from British XXX Corps) and the 11th Armoured (on loan from British VIII Corps) Divisions, began its advance on 15 February through the Hochwald Layback to secure the line of Geldern to Xanten and be situated on the Rhine River's west bank.

On 16 February, the final phase of the battle for the Reichswald Forest began. The 53rd Welsh Division's 71st and 158th Brigades attacked north of the Niers Rivers along the southern edge of the Reichswald Forest to support the 51st Highland Division's assault on Asperden, to Goch's west. The following day, the 53rd's 160th Brigade cleared the narrow sector of farmland between the eastern edge of the Reichswald and the Cleve Forest to join the 51st Highland Division for the Goch attack. The Welshmen had cleared the Reichswald Forest, incurring more than 3,000 casualties.

In Goch, the German garrison, comprising the 180th and 190th Infantry Divisions and the 2nd Parachute Regiment of Straube's LXXXVI Corps, prepared for British XXX Corps' 15th Scottish, 51st Highland and 53rd Welsh three-divisional 18 February attack by utilising pillboxes, minefields, barbed-wire and SPAs of the Siegfried Line's second belt of defences that covered all routes into the fortress town. The 15th Scottish Division mounted its attack to the east of the Niers River, the 51st Highland Division assaulted Goch from the west, with the 53rd Welsh Division in the middle. Hobart's 'Funnies', which included AVREs with bridge-carriers and Petard heavy mortars, were all effectively used against the Nazi defences. Goch, the anchor of the northern Rhineland's Siegfried Line, was taken early on 22 February.

On 19 February, the Canadian 2nd Division joined the combat along the Calcar Road against elements of the German 346th and Panzer *Lehr* Divisions as the Canadian 3rd Division was clearing the Moyland Wood to reach high ground over-looking Calcar. That night, a battle-group of the Panzer *Lehr* Division attacked the Canadian 3rd Division, inflicting steep casualties on two Canadian regiments. At dawn of 20 February, the Panzers resumed their attack to drive the Canadians from Calcar's high ground. However, the timely arrival of Canadian armour from the Fort Garry Horse and the Queen's Own Cameron Highlanders of Canada with AT guns caught the Nazi *Jagdpanthers* in the open. The once-vaunted Panzer *Lehr* Division was broken and retreated south to refit.

On 23 February, Canadian First Army's right wing, British XXX Corps, moved south towards US Ninth Army's now extant Roer River crossing, thus compelling the Nazis to retreat from the Maas River. The 53rd Welsh Division advanced south from Goch to move onto Weeze, reaching the town's ringed AT ditch by nightfall on 24 February. By 0300 hours on 25 February, the Germans lost control of the AT ditch and Allied armour was breaking into Weeze. Later that evening, other 53rd Welsh Division units crossed the Niers River 2 miles south of Weeze, threatening to cut-off the German defenders, which compelled the enemy to withdraw from the fortress town. British XXX Corps continued its southward movement from Weeze to rendezvous at Geldern with the US Ninth Army after the latter formation had suc-cessfully crossed the Roer River.

Montgomery's Operation Veritable cleared the northern sector of the Rhineland between and Maas and Rhine Rivers. However, in the process, Crerar's Canadian First Army, with its British and Canadian contingents, was temporarily bludgeoned by the combat between the Maas and Rhine Rivers in the Reichswald Forest and along the Cleve-Goch-Weeze-Udem-Calcar axis of advance. In Veritable's two weeks of combat, the Canadian First Army sustained 6,000 casualties, of which 4,800 were British, with the heaviest incidence of killed and wounded in the Reichswald Forest action. However, Operation Veritable and the fortnight's delay in beginning the US Ninth Army's Operation Grenade drew nine German divisions into the northern Rhineland combat effectively weakening Nazi defences along the Roer River for the upcoming American crossings there.

Operation Grenade

Before Operation Grenade's intended start date of 9 February, the Roermond Triangle in the British Second Army zone and the seven Roer dams in the US First Army sector had to be seized, both to control the river's water level and prevent any outflanking of the US Ninth Army's start line. Second British Army's XII Corps, under Lieutenant-General Neil Ritchie, attacked the Roermond Triangle on 15 January 1945. Despite a brisk defence by two dug-in German divisions, the two British infantry divisions and one armoured division broke through after gruesome combat. By 25 January, the Roermond Triangle was no longer a threat to the US Ninth Army's flank for the originally planned start date of Operation Grenade on 9 February.

The seven Roer River dams in the US 12th AG's sector were attacked by Hodges' First Army through minefields, sabotaged forests and snow-filled ravines in early February. These Roer River dams controlled over 100 million cubic metres of water. An upstream dam, the Urft, was quickly captured by US troops, but engineers found the discharge valves destroyed, which enabled waters of the Urft reservoir to flow to a downstream dam, the Schwammenauel. A US First Army division attacked the Schwammenauel dam on 5 February. However, German pillboxes and defences along this area of the Siegfried Line's rugged terrain enabled continued Nazi possession of the dam until 9 February – US Ninth Army's intended Roer River assault date. By midnight of 9 February, American engineers reached the Schwammenauel and again found that the enemy had blown the discharge valves, resulting in a steady flow of the reservoir's waters to create a persistent flood into the Roer Valley downstream across the entire US Ninth Army's front. Simpson's divisions were to wait until 23 February for the Roer's waters to recede. During this fortnight, the Germans sent their reserve formations to the north to combat the Canadian First Army during Operation Veritable.

Allied planners anticipated that the Roer River dams would be emptied by 24 February, with the waterway's level dropping sufficiently for bridging. However, Simpson calculated that if Operation Grenade commenced one day before the water level had finally fallen, the Americans might catch the Nazi defenders unaware. Therefore, the US Ninth Army was ordered to cross the Roer River with twenty-eight infantry battalions at 0330 hours on 23 February, following an hour-long, 1,000-gun preparatory bombardment by the combined artillery of the US Ninth and British Second Armies.

Three US Corps were deployed along a 30-mile-wide front. On the left was Major-General Alvan Gillem's XIII Corps, which had its infantry divisions – the 102nd in the Linnich area and the 84th 4 miles to the north. Behind the infantry, 15 miles back at Heerlen, was the US 5th Armoured Division. XIII Corps was to cross the Roer and seize the Huckelhoven-Ratheim-Golkrath triangle. In the centre was Major-General Raymond S. McClain's XIX Corps with two divisions, the 30th Division comprising the southern flank and the 29th Division to the north opposite Julich. Towards the rear, McClain had placed his 83rd Division as a corps reserve along with the US 2nd Armoured Division, situated near Aachen, to exploit a breakthrough. Further to the south on Grenade's right flank was Major-General J. Lawton Collins' VII Corps (on loan from the US First Army), which participated in the Roer River crossing at Duren with the 8th and 84th Infantry Divisions, which were to link-up with the XIX Corps to the east of Julich.

On the US Ninth Army's northern flank was Major-General John Anderson's XVI Corps. This formation was new and unbloodied, being comprised of the US 8th Armoured, 79th Infantry and 35th Infantry Divisions. XVI Corps was not going to cross the Roer because of its lack of river assault combat experience. Instead, it was to drive north along the river's west bank to clear any remnant Nazi positions and only cross unopposed before it advanced northwards to clear the east bank of the Maas River towards Venlo and meet the Canadian First Army heading south from Goch towards Geldern.

Opposing the Americans were only elements of the German 8th Parachute Division, as most of this formation had reinforced the Moyland Wood on the Cleve-Calcar Road to battle II Canadian Corps in the northern Rhineland. Other German formations included the 59th and 176th Infantry Divisions and the 183rd and 363rd *Volksgrenadier* Divisions. Notwithstanding the German troop depletions, the enemy's defence was tenacious with resistance at each Roer riverside village and town. The Germans responded with artillery, mortars and occasional dive-bomber sorties to disrupt both the assault craft and heavier bridge-building.

The raging Roer River tossed many assault craft and caused many to reach the east bank far from their intended destinations. Despite US Ninth Army suffering over a thousand casualties on the initial day of the crossing, bridge-building across the turbulent Roer River was a priority to expand the bridgehead. Seven tank-bearing bridges were constructed as a Nazi counter-attack failed to materialise. The Roer River crossings were at locales that the Germans rated unsuitable, which aided the element of surprise. Amid weakening German defence as well as piecemeal reserve formations' commitment to the battle, the US Ninth Army vectored north-eastward for a rendezvous with the British and Canadians, first at Geldern, after which both armies started their movements eastwards to converge towards the west bank of the Rhine River.

As so many German units were dispatched to the north against the Canadian First Army during Operation Veritable, the US Ninth Army faced token opposition. Simpson's 2nd Armoured Division reached the Rhine at Neuss on 2 March. However, the Germans destroyed the railroad bridge there, which spanned the river towards Dusseldorf on the east bank. Another bridge at Oberkassel, a few miles downstream, was assaulted in a *coup de main* by a small US 83rd Division column. However, when the attack was discovered by German sentries, the sentries had destroyed the bridge.

On 28 February, Collins' VII Corps crossed the Erft River and began vectoring towards Cologne, Germany's fifth largest city situated on the Rhine River. By 5 March, VII Corps armour broke into Cologne, with its cathedral intact despite the locale's aerial destruction. On 7 March, Cologne fell to VII Corps. However, the city's link to the eastern bank of the Rhine River, the 1200-foot segment of the Hohenzollern Bridge had been destroyed the previous day, making a river crossing over that structure impossible.

Operation Blockbuster

Operation Blockbuster began on 26 February, which coincided with the US Ninth Army's north-eastward movement. The Canadian First Army's left wing comprised Simonds' II Canadian Corps and augmented with some British XXX and VIII Corps units. The Canadian 2nd and 3rd Divisions moved rapidly from their start line of the Goch-Calcar Road in *Kangaroo* APCs led by armour and artillery. Crerar planned this offensive across the plateau between Calcar and Udem after the fall of Goch as the final phase of the Canadian First Army's movement to the Rhine River.

The German First Parachute Army commander, Schlemm, directed his two corps commanders, von Luttwitz and Meindl, to mount a tenacious defence in this sector. Against fierce German resistance, the II Canadian Corps forced a passage through Udem, but a bitter struggle ensued against the Hochwald Forest's fortifications, which halted the Canadian offensive from capturing Xanten (called the 'Gateway to the Rhine'). The two main roads leading to Xanten crossed the Hochwald Forest, with the Goch-to-Xanten railway embankment bisecting it. Nazi defences in the forest were covered by a triple trench system, each one-third of a mile apart, which had minefields and barbed-wire protecting them. Behind an escarpment stretching from Calcar to Udem's east were further AT ditches, pillboxes, wire entanglements, and 88mm AT guns salvaged from the Siegfried Line. The Hochwald Forest and its approaches gave excellent fields of fire to the German gunners and proved to be more effective than the concrete defences in the Siegfried Line and the fortifications in the Reichswald Forest. Canadian infantry were forced to disembark from their

Kangaroo APCs after being shelled by the German 88mm AT guns, and they advanced amid the trees and wet terrain.

On 2 March, the II Canadian Corps broke through the escarpment's gap and the Hochwald Forest after five days of combat and approached Xanten. The 43rd Wessex Division made an easier advance through Calcar and headed for Xanten. German troops retreated to Xanten to avoid encirclement and capture. Once Xanten was taken, the two 400-yard-long Rhine bridges spanning the river to Wesel were doomed. Wesel was an important road, rail and river traffic centre and ideally situated for the Allied armies to break-out into the north German plain as well as envelop the Ruhr industrial region from the north.

It was uncertain as to why Crerar attacked Xanten across the heavily defended ground, as British XXX Corps was about to move eastwards to outflank both the 'Gateway to the Rhine and the Hochwald Forest. This XXX Corps movement by itself would have compelled Schlemm to withdraw his forces in the II Canadian Corps zone. However, Hitler insisted that there was to be no withdrawal across the Rhine to the east bank as Xanten's garrison was instructed to fight to the last man.

The tide's final turn against the Germans in the northern Rhineland to the west of the Rhine River barrier occurred during the afternoon of 2 March, when elements of the US Ninth Army's 35th Division were in possession of Geldern and about to meet the 53rd Welsh Division's 158th Brigade. A continuous 21st AG front was soon to turn north-eastwards from Kevelaer and advance on a Geldern-to-Alpen axis to the Rhine River.

Until 10 March, 21st AG continued their attacks on the German First Parachute Army trapped on the west bank opposite Wesel. The 21st AG casualties for the northern Rhineland campaign numbered almost 23,000, of which two-thirds were incurred by the bludgeoned Canadian First Army, with 5,300 Canadian and 10,300 British casualties, along with some from Dempsey's British Second Army. American forces suffered 7,300 casualties during the Roer River crossing and north-eastern drive to the Rhine River.

To emphasise the enemy's tenacity, there were 90,000 German casualties among the numerous Nazi divisions defending the northern Rhineland in order to protect the industrial Ruhr region for the Third Reich's Nazi war machine to the east of the Rhine River. The German First Parachute Army was mauled and Schlemm pleaded with von Rundstedt to grant permission for the withdrawal of his surviving battered nine combat divisions to the Rhine River's east bank. On 5 March Schlemm, who Hitler made personally responsible for not allowing the Rhine bridges in his sector to fall into Allied hands, ordered all crossing sites destroyed except for the one at Wesel, which he intended to defend to the last. On 6 March, Schlemm began evacuating troops and equipment as fast as he could to the east bank, with a rear-guard maintaining the truncating perimeter. Finally, at 0700 hours on 10 March, the railway bridge across the Rhine at Wesel was destroyed with as many German troops as possible crossing to the east bank.

Montgomery was not going to mount a sudden operation for 21st AG to 'bounce the Rhine'. Instead, he orchestrated an elaborate plan, Operation Plunder, a set-piece crossing of the river barrier, with amphibious craft and air support. An airborne landing, Operation Varsity, on the east bank was to occur simultaneously with the amphibious river crossing. After that, Montgomery planned for a strike into the Ruhr region and then north onto Berlin and the Baltic.

US 12th Army Group drive to the Rhine

The US First and Third Armies closed the 'bulge' in the Ardennes with their winter counter-offensive. With the shift of the US Ninth Army to Montgomery's 21st AG, Bradley's 12th AG initially took a more subsidiary role in the Ruhr region's eventual capture. As part of Eisenhower's 'broad front strategy', Bradley's divisions were tasked with an advance into the Schnee Eifel mountains, a forested region contiguous with the Ardennes and bordering the Rhineland, beyond which lay the Moselle River and the confluence with the Rhine.

From 28 January to 1 February 1945, the US First and Third Armies tried to pierce the German defences near the Losheim Gap, to the north-east of St Vith. Deep snow, icy roads and traffic congestion delayed the American advance. By 1 February, only the initial outlying pillbox defences of the Siegfried Line had been reached. Adding to Bradley's logistic dilemmas, Eisenhower shifted additional 12th AG divisions to Simpson's US Ninth Army.

Hodges' US First Army advanced to seize the Roer River dams and also protect US Ninth Army's right flank. On 30 January, the Americans launched an attack towards the Urft dam, at the weakest part of the German LXXIV Corps sector. For several days, fierce combat ensued. However, the US 7th Armoured and 78th and 9th Infantry Divisions broke through the lines of the German 62nd *Volksgrenadier* Division, as German Fifteenth Army leader, von Zangen, under Model's AG B command, scoured his sector for reserve battalions to contest the American thrust. American troops combated the German concrete fortifications supported by heavy Panzers. The US First Army units were hampered at capturing the Urft and Schwammenauel dams intact before massive amounts of water were diverted, in part, due to a lack of requisite strength. Some of Hodges' armour and artillery units were sent to support Patton's Third Army while infantry formations were diverted to Simpson's Ninth Army.

Patton's Third Army drive commenced on 3 March with Lieutenant-General Troy Middleton's VIII Corps moving against stout Nazi resistance eastward from Prüm and Lieutenant Manton Eddy's XII Corps rapidly crossing the Kyll river to Bitburg's east. Two days later, Patton's vaunted 4th Armoured Division, under the command of

Major-General Hugh Gaffey, swung north-east ahead of the infantry towards the Rhine River about a dozen miles beyond the Kyll. Several thousand Germans surrendered to the Americans in the armoured thrust. On 6 March, Patton's armour was halfway between the Kyll and Rhine Rivers. In an area north of the Moselle and west of the Rhine Rivers, Germans flocked with little unit cohesion towards the latter waterway in search of a crossing to the east bank.

After receiving an additional armoured division, the Third Army captured Trier and thrusted eastward into the Saar region, clearing the north bank of the Moselle, and moving towards the Rhine on a line from Mainz to Mannheim.

US 6th AG drive to the Rhine

Lieutenant-General Jacob Devers' 6th AG, comprising the US Seventh Army and the First French Army, was charged with reducing the 'Colmar Pocket', an area on the Rhine's west bank to the south of Strasbourg and in the vicinity of Germany's Black Forest. In bitter combat from the end of January 1945 to 5 February, which involved five American and six French divisions, the Allies suffered 18,000 casualties. Hitler allowed von Rundstedt to extricate the battered German Nineteenth Army across the Rhine after suffering more than 30,000 casualties. By 9 February, the west bank of the Rhine south of Strasbourg was devoid of enemy troops.

Rhine River crossing on the Ludendorff Railway Bridge, Remagen

The Remagen Bridgehead Operation occurred on 7–17 March. At 2300 hours on 6 March, Major-General John Milliken, commander of US First Army's III Corps, pointed to a map reference, the Ludendorff Railway Bridge over the Rhine at the German town of Remagen, and told his 9th Armored Division commanding general, the First World War-decorated Major-General John Leonard, that he would be famous if he captured the structure intact. Since the Nazi high command had been destroying all of the bridges across the Rhine to prevent their capture and an ensuing bridgehead for the Allies, it was foreseen by SHAEF that an amphibious river-crossing operation would be necessary, but not in the First Army sector containing Remagen. Milliken had previously received orders from Hodges and Bradley on 3 March that III Corps' objective was to cross the Ahr River in order to link up with US Third Army. However, Milliken and his divisional commanders wanted to reach the Rhine and the corps commander planned a movement against the Rhine on either side of Bonn with only the 9th Armoured Division moving towards the Ahr.

General von Zangen's Fifteenth Army staff was at odds with SHAEF's assessment and believed that the advancing Americans would take advantage of the open terrain of the Rheinbach Valley towards the Ahr River and then onto the Rhine. He described the shape of the suspected advance of the Americans as that of a funnel with Remagen at the end. However, AG B commander Model, in keeping with

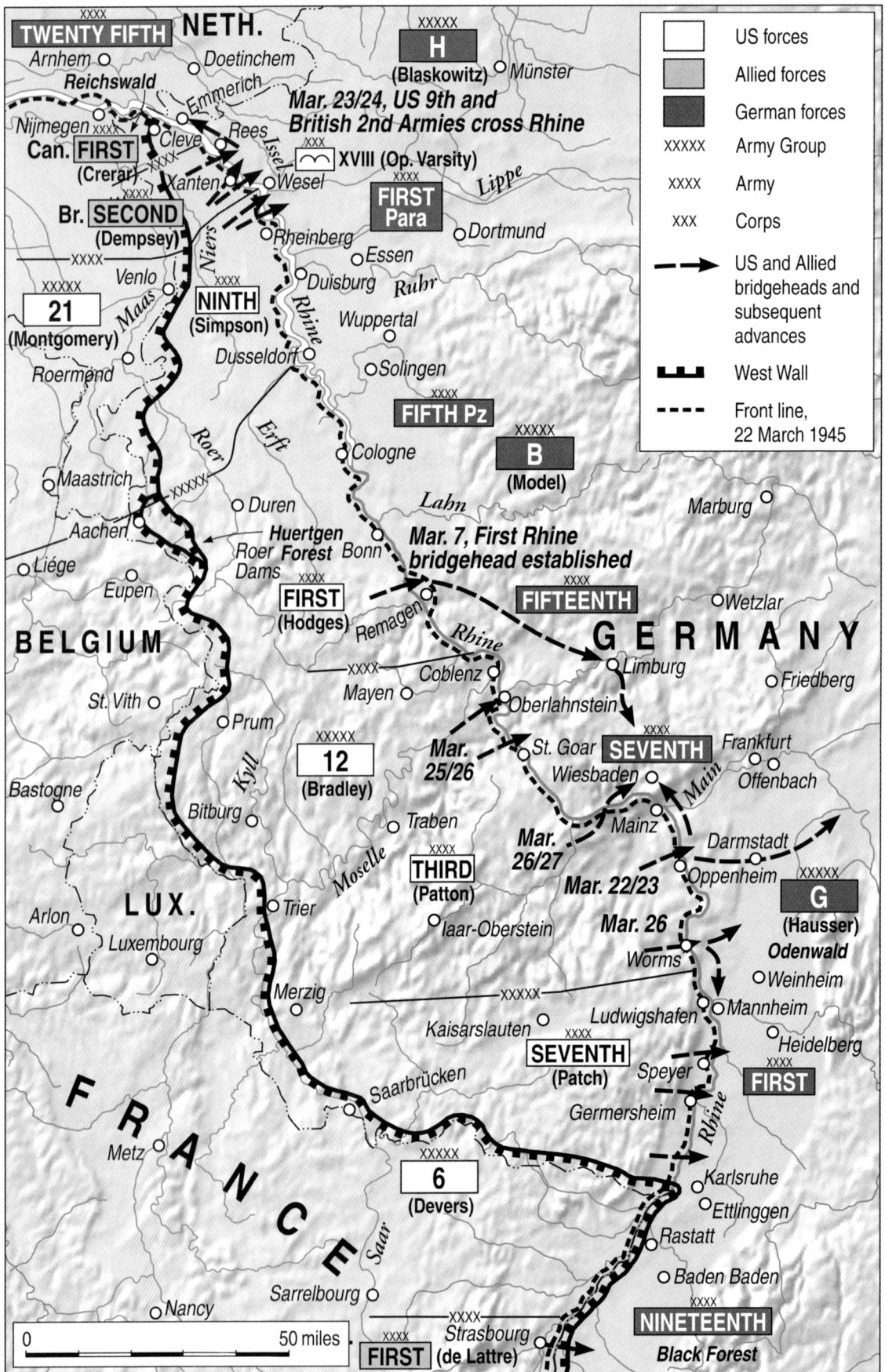

TWENTY FIFTH

NETH.

H
(Blaskowitz)

Arnhem
Doetinchem
Münster

Reichswald

Nijmegen
Emmerich
Cleve
Rees
Mar. 23/24, US 9th and
British 2nd Armies cross Rhine

Can. FIRST
(Crerar)
Xanten
Wesel
XVIII (Op. Varsity)

Br. SECOND
(Dempsey)
Niers
Rheinberg
FIRST
Para
Dortmund

Venlo
Duisburg
Essen

21
(Montgomery)
Maas
NINTH
(Simpson)
Rhine
Ruhr
Wuppertal

Roermond
Dusseldorf
Solingen

Roer
Erft
FIFTH Pz

Maastrich
Duren
Cologne
B
(Model)

Aachen
Huertgen
Forest
Roer
Dams
Bonn
Lahn
Mar. 7, First Rhine
bridgehead established
Marburg

Liége
Eupen

BELGIUM
FIRST
(Hodges)
Remagen
FIFTEENTH
Wetzlar

GERMANY

St. Vith
Prum
Mayen
Coblenz
Rhine
Limburg
Friedberg

12
(Bradley)
Oberlahnstein
Mar.
25/26
St. Goar
SEVENTH
Wiesbaden
Frankfurt

Bastogne
Bitburg
Kyll
Traben
Mainz
Main
Offenbach

THIRD
(Patton)
Moselle
Mar.
26/27
Mar. 22/23
Darmstadt
Oppenheim
G
(Hausser)

Arlon
LUX.
Trier
Iaar-Oberstein
Mar. 26
Worms
Odenwald
Weinheim

Luxembourg
Merzig
Ludwigshafen
Mannheim
Heidelberg

FRANCE
Kaisarslauten
SEVENTH
(Patch)
Speyer
Rhine
FIRST

Metz
Saarbrücken
Germersheim

6
(Devers)
Karlsruhe
Ettlinggen

Saar
Rastatt
Baden Baden

Nancy
Sarrelbourg
Strasbourg
NINETEENTH

FIRST (de Lattre)
Black Forest

0   50 miles

US forces
Allied forces
German forces
xxxxx Army Group
xxxx   Army
xxx   Corps
US and Allied
bridgeheads and
subsequent
advances
West Wall
Front line,
22 March 1945

the American planners, realised that it was folly to cross the Rhine at Remagen where the cliffs rose steeply on the opposite bank and believed the likely assault locale would be Bonn. Therefore, Model refused to reinforce von Zangen, who was in charge of the Remagen sector, with a request of two German corps to protect the Ludendorff Bridge. The railway bridge was left defended by a handful of engineers, members of the local *Volkssturm*, and a few infantrymen. It proved to be a fatal oversight.

US III Corps' 9th Armoured Division under Leonard moved 'down the funnel' to Remagen on 6 March with a mixed task-force of tanks, infantry and supporting vehicles – led by Brigadier-General William Hoge. Hoge's previous combat experience included leading engineering formations on D-Day at *Omaha* Beach to clear obstacles while under fire as well as leading the 9th Armored Division's CCB during the Ardennes campaign. General von Zangen's attempts to slow III Corps' movement were futile, as many elements of Fifteenth Army were withdrawn towards Bonn late on 6 March, making Remagen an even easier target.

Hoge's initial orders focused on a south-east movement towards the Ahr River, a western tributary of the Rhine a few miles south of Remagen, and made no reference to taking the Ludendorff Railway Bridge or to gaining a bridgehead to the Rhine's east. By the afternoon of 6 March, CCB moved towards the Ahr River and cleared the enemy from the town of Meckenheim. Hoge's units were within a day's trek to the Rhine River in the vicinity of Sinzig and Remagen. On this day, a 9th Armoured Division scout plane flew over the Ludendorff Railway Bridge and reported that it was

---

The Allied 'Broad Front' Rhine River assaults. The Allied armies' crossings of the Rhine River from Rees in the north to Strasbourg in the south are shown. With extensive preparation and artillery bombardment, Montgomery's 21st AG (British Second and US Ninth Armies crossings) occurred on 23–24 March against Rees, Wesel and the river's east bank opposite Rheinberg. A coincident airborne assault was also launched on 24 March, Operation *Varsity*, by the US XVIII Airborne Corps (US 17th and British 6th Airborne Divisions and the attached 1st Canadian Parachute Battalion). A weakened German AG H, under Blaskowitz, comprising the *Luftwaffe's* First Parachute Army, resisted the Rhine River crossings. US First Army's III Corps units had previously crossed the Rhine at Remagen on 7 March over the captured Ludendorff Railway Bridge. After expanding the bridgehead, these forces moved south along the Rhine towards Coblenz to eventually link-up with Patton's Third Army. German AG B, under Model, defended against the US 12th AG American. Further to the south, Patton hurried his XII Corps' crossing of the river at Oppenheim on the night of 22–23 March before Montgomery's offensive began. Subsequent crossings were carried out on 25–26 March at Oberlahnstein and St Goar. During the early hours of 26 March, US Seventh Army guns heralded the US 45th and 3rd Divisions' crossing of the Rhine just to the north of Worms. German opposition was mounted by Hausser's AG G. However, it quickly broke down with the US 45th and 3rd Divisions pursuing the vanquished enemy in the vicinity of the Odenwald. North African elements of the French First Army essentially devoid of logistic support to mount a river crossing nonetheless attacked from the vicinity of Strasbourg before moving in the direction of Stuttgart. (*Meridian Mapping*)

not yet destroyed. At 0330 hours on 7 March, Leonard's 9th Armored Division HQ changed CCB's mission as it moved beyond Meckenheim's rubble. Leonard ordered CCB to advance to the west bank of the Rhine in two columns – a northern one, under Lieutenant-Colonel Engemann, aimed at seizing both Remagen and Kripp, and a southern one responsible for Sinzig's capture – in addition to securing bridgeheads over the Ahr River. Engemann's CCB column arrived at Remagen just past noon on 7 March. To avoid radio interception, Hoge sent Major Ben Cothran to Engemann's northern column of CCB with orders to take the bridge if it were still standing.

Engemann's northern column comprised the 9th Armoured Division's 14th TB and units from the 27th Armoured Infantry Battalion. By the time Cothran reached this northern column, it had already cleared the nearby woods of the enemy and Engemann was ecstatic as he overlooked with his binoculars the still intact Ludendorff Railway Bridge through the morning fog. One part of the bridge was converted with wood planking into a motor road bridge and German vehicles moved across it to the east bank of the Rhine River. German troops on the bridge were not feverishly preparing to detonate explosives to demolish it. Along the river's east bank's railway line, a locomotive pulled a string of freight cars.

Engeman quickly summoned a platoon of the 14th Tank Battalion's Company A's new M26 Pershing tanks, with their 90mm guns. At 1320 hours, Engemann also instructed Company A of the 27th Armored Infantry Battalion, led by Lieutenant Karl Timmermann, to go through the town of Remagen and reach the bridge on foot while accompanying the armour. The *ad hoc* American assault force left the cover of the woods and twisted down a steep, tree-lined road into Remagen. The platoon of Pershing tanks approached the western end of the bridge between 1430–1500 hours before the infantry, having encountered no AT resistance from the Germans while coursing through Remagen. Lieutenant Grimball's platoon of M26 tanks knocked out the train across the river. Hoge himself arrived and saw first-hand the opportunity to seize this intact bridge midway between Bonn and Coblenz and urged his infantry through the town to the river.

Timmermann's armoured infantry observed the tanks moving toward the bridge, so his company followed the descending main road running south-west through the centre of the town towards the river's span. Timmermann deployed his company into three platoons and moved towards the western side's twin bridge abutment towers. Under German rifle-fire, Timmermann led his soldiers past the few remaining houses along the river and now observed German engineers preparing to detonate explosives.

As the American tanks and infantry approached the bridge, the local German commanders, Major Scheller and Captain Friesenhahn of the Ludendorff Railway Bridge's defence detachment, finished inspecting the demolitions at the western end of the bridge. Within minutes of their inspection, Captain Friesenhahn ordered a charge detonated under the approach ramp to the western side of the bridge. The ensuing explosion along the causeway near the western end of the bridge produced a plume of dirt and cobblestones that rose into the air and cratered the road with a 30-foot hole, intended to keep American tanks from gaining access to the bridge's western end. This large hole in the causeway leading up to the bridge seemed capable of stopping armoured vehicles, but not the assaulting American infantrymen.

Scheller and Friesenhahn retreated to the eastern side of the bridge and, after some ineffective communication, the former ordered the engineers to set-off the main detonator circuit near the tunnel entrance, which controlled the demolitions for the centre and eastern spans of the Ludendorff Railway Bridge. This main detonator circuit failed. However, a valiant German soldier ran about 100 yards onto the bridge to manually set-off the primer cord to a secondary circuit controlling the charges on the eastern portion of the bridge at the stone pier. There soon followed another explosion two-thirds of the way across the bridge's span with wooden planks rising into the air. The bridge seemed to lift up. However, it settled with the structure still intact. It was entirely unclear to the German officers why the explosives did not detonate properly and send the bridge crashing into the Rhine. Afterwards, American engineers found a problem with the placement of the blasting cap to detonate the entire array of demolitions.

At 1512 hours, the Pershing tanks, still at the western end of the bridge, started covering it with MG-fire. Lieutenant Timmermann prodded his three infantry platoons across the bridge despite enemy MG-fire from the towers on the eastern side of the bridge and from a barge in the river. American tank-fire neutralised these German positions, which was crucial for Timmerman's armoured infantry to capture both of the towers and continue crossing the bridge. As Timmermann's troops raced across the bridge, they cut any wires they saw and threw the explosives into the river.

Three members of the 9th Armoured Engineer Battalion dashed onto the bridge with the assault infantry to cut demolition wires, which prevented the Nazis from detonating a large charge planted on the bridge's cross-beams underneath. The combat engineers located a 500lb charge of TNT about two-thirds of the way across the river. The blasting cap had gone off, but the charge failed to explode. Other engineers found 350-pound charges, which had not exploded on the bridge's piers as American artillery may have severed one of the cables leading to the demolitions.

American artillery and mortars fired white phosphorus into the town on the east bank of the river, driving the Nazi defenders into the railway tunnel's cover to avoid the incendiary shells. The remainder of the 27th Armoured Infantry Battalion's troops arrived at the bridge, dismounted from their half-tracks and went into firing position downstream from the bridge. Timmermann and a handful of his men reached the far side of the bridge with more than 100 men crossing the Ludendorff Bridge by late afternoon. By 1700 hours, Timmermann and his infantrymen cleared the hill and reached the eastern end of the tunnel. Sergeant Alex Drabik was credited as the first soldier across the bridge followed by Timmermann and the rest of his assault company. Drabik and Timmermann, along with some other infantrymen and combat engineers, were awarded Distinguished Service Crosses for their actions at the Ludendorff Railway Bridge on 7 March.

The recently appointed German commander, Major Scheller, escaped on a bicycle from the eastern side of the tunnel before Timmermann's arrival to report to the *Wehrmacht's* Fifteenth Army's HQ that the intact bridge was in American hands. Also, a *Luftwaffe* officer still at the bridge's tunnel, Captain Willi Bratge, sent a message to German High Command that the bridge's demolition was unsuccessful with the Americans in possession of the span and on the Rhine River's east bank. Then, Bratge instructed his men to surrender to the Americans on both sides of the tunnel.

By 2200 hours, three American rifle companies (A, B and C) of the 27th Armoured Infantry Battalion, each with many casualties, occupied the Rhine's eastern shore. This force was sufficient to beat back a German counter-attack comprising engineers and anti-aircraft crews near Erpeler Ley ('Flak Hill'). The counter-attacking Germans were carrying 1,000lb of explosive with them to destroy the bridge. Some US M4 tanks, which were narrower than the M26 Pershing tanks, were able to crawl at a slow speed across a bridge led by infantrymen acting as guides with the bridge's surface being 'pockmarked' by the day's earlier fighting. After the failed Nazi counter-attack on the east side of the Rhine; Timmermann's Company A, 27th Armored Infantry Battalion, turned downstream towards Erpel to ascend the cliffs there while Company B took the cliffs immediately above the bridge. Company C moved onto Orsberg.

Late on 7 March, to avoid German sniper fire, bulldozers slowly filled the crater on the western ramp of the bridge. American infantrymen took lumber from nearby house exteriors to put a new wooden surface over the rail planks destroyed earlier to the centre and eastern spans. The bridge repairs were completed by midnight and enabled the Americans to establish one-way vehicular traffic.

Overnight, the 14th Tank Battalion's Company A crossed the bridge and set-up a road block. The 52nd Armored Infantry Battalion crossed the bridge and established its command post at Erpel, taking over the northern half of the perimeter on the east side of the Rhine. Also, during the night of 7–8 March, the roads to the west and south of Remagen were clogged with reinforcements, initially of CCB and then other US III Corps units, rushed up by Milliken

At dawn on 8 March, the 1st Battalion, 310th Infantry, crossed the Ludendorff Railway Bridge and occupied the high ground south of the bridge around Ockenfels in order to prohibit the Germans from using this village as an observation post for German artillery to bombard the bridge. Also, that morning, the remaining armour of the 14th Tank Battalion, minus Company A, crossed the bridge and went into mobile reserve. During the remaining daylight hours of that day, the 9th Infantry Division's

47th Regiment and the 78th Division's 311th Regiment crossed the Rhine and took up perimeter positions to the east and north-east of the 27th and 52nd Armored Infantry Battalions. The 99th Infantry Division was also ordered to exploit the 9th Armoured Division's seizure of the Ludendorff Bridge. These crossings occurred during almost continuous German artillery fire on the bridge and bridgehead.

The Americans had intercepted German radio traffic ordering a heavy bombing raid on the bridge the following day. However, bad weather caused the mission to be aborted. The American *coup de main* had unintentionally carved out a bridgehead 1 mile deep and 2 miles wide on the eastern side of the Rhine.

Allied movements after the Remagen bridgehead

Hitler summoned GFM Kesselring to Berlin on 9 March. The C-in-C Italy was to replace von Rundstedt as C-in-C West. Hitler raged at von Runstedt for both the Remagen debacle as well as the Wesel bridgehead being evacuated by Schlemm in the face of the British-Canadian drive to the Rhine River. It was von Rundstedt's last firing by the *Führer*. The Germans had fifty-five half-strength divisions against eighty-five Allied ones from northern Germany to the Swiss border. Kesselring marshalled the *Luftwaffe* forces in the west to destroy the American bridgehead at Remagen by almost non-stop bombing of the Ludendorff Railway Bridge and the temporary tactical bridges and ferries erected by US combat engineers to reinforce the east bank of the Rhine River. RAF Hawker Tempests, which had the requisite range from Dutch airfields to the Remagen bridgehead, sortied against the *Luftwaffe's* aerial assaults. V-2 rockets and a few 4,400lb rounds from their railway-mounted, 130-ton Morser Karl were also unleashed to bombard the Ludendorff Railway Bridge. On 11 March, Kesselring conferred with Model, Blaskowitz, von Zangen and Schlemm to review the dire German circumstances.

The Ludendorff Railway Bridge finally collapsed into the Rhine on 17 March. Other American pontoon bridges had been erected to handle US First Army's flow of *matériel* onto the Rhine's east bank. Thus, with the Remagen bridgehead still expanding, Eisenhower continued to implement Montgomery's plan for a major 21st AG operation to cross the Rhine to the Ruhr region's north.

As the Allied Rhine River crossing at Remagen lured several piecemeal German counter-attacks onto the bridgehead, Patton unleashed his Third Army assault into the Saar-Palatinate region on 12 March with a corps-sized eastward movement from Trier, just beyond the now-pierced Siegfried Line. Two days later, Eddy's XII Corps crossed the lower Moselle along a southward thrust into the Saar region to cut off the German First Army and get further behind the Siegfried Line defences. On 16 March, Patton sent a third corps across the Moselle River between the XII Corps and Trier. German AG G commander, General Hausser, rushed under-strength divisions from his Nineteenth Army, battered by combat in the 'Colmar Pocket'.

Kesselring feared that large numbers of his forces were to be encircled on the west bank of the Rhine. On 20 March, German General Felber was given permission to withdraw his Seventh Army across the Rhine. On 22 March, the US Third and Seventh Armies linked up with the two American formations, collectively capturing approximately 100,000 Germans. Patton had successfully penetrated through the Saar-Palatinate and deprived the Germans of this industrial region, making them wholly dependent on the war resources of the Ruhr. The next day, Hitler finally relented and gave orders to withdraw across the Rhine. However, most Germans had already done so.

By the third week of March, Patton's XII Corps completed the clearance of the west bank of the Rhine of German forces with only Nazi stragglers remaining there. To the Germans, the most logical place for a US Third Army crossing was north of Mainz at the confluence of the Main and Rhine Rivers, thereby nullifying a second crossing of the Main River. However, Patton opted for a *coup de main* to avoid antici-pated German defences, so he directed Eddy's XIIth Corps to feign a crossing near Mainz with one division, and instead cross 10 miles upstream at Oppenheim with the experienced river assault forces of the US 5th Infantry Division, under Major-General Leroy Irwin. Patton was determined to cross the Rhine not later than 22–23 March, the night before Montgomery's massive, set-piece Operations Plunder, Widgeon and Varsity were to unfold.

At 2200 hours on 22 March, 5th Division assault battalions in boats paddled across the Rhine at Nierstein and Oppenheim. There was no preparatory artillery bombard-ment to heighten surprise. There were limited German defenders opposing the 5th Division's crossing and only a few American casualties were incurred in the two-hour river assault. Then, combat engineers constructed treadway bridges across the river and exit ramps for subsequent waves of DUKWs. By the end of 23 March, the entire 5th Division was across the Rhine and a second infantry division was crossing. Tanks and TDs were ferried over on LCVPs. Eddy ordered an armoured division to the east bank on 24 March.

Enemy resistance to the US XII Corps crossing was limited to artillery fire and occasional *Luftwaffe* sorties. The German Seventh Army, between Mainz to Mannheim, fielded only headquarters, rear-echelon and auxiliary forces in less than divisional strength. A German counter-attack against American forces on the Rhine's east bank was mounted by officer candidate students from nearby Wiesbaden. The link between German Seventh Army north of the Main River and the German First Army south of Mannheim was severed.

Later, US Third Army crossings by VIII and XX Corps were to occur south of the Moselle at St Goar and Oberwesel between Mainz and Coblenz. German opposition comprising elements of LXXXIV Corps, with a division of 400 infantr-ymen, a collection of *Volkssturm*, and assorted Howitzers and AA artillery pieces, which were unable to deter Middleton's VIII Corps' 87th and 89th Infantry Divisions' crossings. By 26 March, Allied reconnaissance aircraft noted Nazi motorised units fleeing east on clogged roads. Near the Lahn River, Third and First Armies were to link-up on the Rhine River's east bank.

The stage was now set for Montgomery's Rhine River crossings in the north. However, on the night of 23 March, Bradley announced Patton's 5th Division crossing of the Rhine River to war correspondents. He emphasised competitively that American forces crossed the river without aerial bombardment or an airborne assault.

British XXX Corps infantry and armour are amassed along a wooded path to Nijmegen's east to commence the Canadian First Army's Operation Veritable on 8 February. Massive aerial and artillery bombardment stunned the Nazi defenders of Schlemm's German First Parachute Army in the Reichswald Forest area. However, floods, muddy terrain and vehicular congestion were to hamper the speed with which Horrocks' XXX Corps was to move onto Cleve and beyond. (*Author's Collection*)

A British XXX Corps infantryman pulls down a Nazi flag with his bayonet in heavily bombarded Cleve, a principal early target of Operation Veritable situated to the Reichswald Forest's north-east on the vital northern Rhineland road, connecting Nijmegen and Nutterden to the west with Calcar to the south-east. Once Cleve was neutralised, Allied infantry divisions and supporting armour were to move south on to Goch to the Reichswald Forest's south-east. With areas of the Nijmegen-Cleve road under floodwaters along with massive vehicular congestion from mud and bomb craters, Cleve's capture was delayed by over four days. (*NARA*)

(**Opposite, above**) A line of M4 medium tanks (Sherman Fireflies) bombard enemy positions in the Reichswald Forest area to the east of Nijmegen at the start of Operation Veritable on 8 February. This M4 was a variant of a QF 17-pounder (3-inch or 76.2mm) AT gun, which was capable of penetrating Panzer V (Panther) and VI (Tiger) armour. The M4 variant was available to Montgomery's 21st AG during the Normandy and Ardennes campaigns. (*NARA*)

(**Opposite, below**) Infantrymen from the British XXX Corps' 51st Highland Division disembarking wooden assault boats after crossing the winding terrain obstacle of the Niers River on 13–14 February. Other divisional units crossed south of Hekkens, where a bridge was demolished, in Buffaloes, to move onto Asperden and Goch. The Niers River, a tributary of the Maas River, runs south through Goch, Weeze, Kevelaer and Geldern. (*NARA*)

Advancing 53rd Welsh Division soldiers from the 1st Battalion, Herefordshire Light Infantry Regiment traverse an AT ditch that ringed the entire German town of Udem. Often these temporary defences were overcome with specialised Churchill tanks carrying fascines or bridging sections. The assault was part of the Canadian First Army's late February's Operation Blockbuster, a continued south-east drive after the gruesome combat for Cleve, the Reichswald Forest and Goch. (*Author's Collection*)

(**Opposite, above**) An infantry section of the 4th Battalion, Welch Regiment in British XXX Corps' 53rd Welsh Division cautiously advances, in trench-coats, through the ruins of heavily bombed Weeze, situated to Goch's south-east and Udem's south-west, during late February's Operation Blockbuster. The Canadian First Army moved south after Operation Veritable was completed to rendezvous with the northerly advancing US Ninth Army at Geldern following Operation Grenade's Roer River crossings. (*NARA*)

(**Opposite, below**) A section from the 1st Battalion, Oxfordshire and Buckinghamshire Light Infantry of British XXX Corps' 53rd Welsh Division skirmishes through an intact area of Weeze in late February. Most of Weeze was devastated in a nocturnal RAF bomber raid on 8 February, the start date of Operation Veritable. (*NARA*)

(**Opposite, above**) A line of Kangaroos, Canadian turretless Ram tanks converted into APCs, prepare to transport British XXX Corps infantry. The Allied soldiers were queuing up in order to board them for the assault on Kervenheim to the south of Udem and east of Weeze in early March. (*NARA*)

(**Opposite, below**) An infantry section from the Royal Norfolks from VIII Corps' 3rd Division in Dempsey's British Second Army advances through the ruins of Kervenheim, 3 miles to the south of Udem, on 25 February after stout Nazi resistance finally crumbled. (*NARA*)

(**Above**) A patrol from the 43rd Wessex Division of British XXX Corps, on loan to Simonds' Canadian II Corps, enters Calcar on 28 February, two days after Operation Blockbuster commenced. The town was situated on a main road north of Xanten. Calcar was previously devastated by an RAF bomber raid at the start of Operation Veritable. The British troops advanced into Calcar as units of the Canadian 2nd and 3rd Divisions were battling elements of Schlemm's First Parachute Army defending the Hochwald Gap. (*NARA*)

Infantrymen from the 53rd Welsh Division of British XXX Corps fire at snipers from behind a disabled German artillery piece in Alpen on 10 March. Alpen, situated north-west of Rheinberg and to Xanten's south-east, was along the boundary of the Canadian First and British Second Armies. On this day, the Germans destroyed the bridges over the Rhine River at Wesel to Alpen's north-west. *(NARA)*

By 2 March, after five days of bloodied combat, elements of the Canadian II Corps broke through the Nazi-defended Hochwald Gap and moved onto Xanten, the final German locale before the Rhine River. Canadian 2nd Division's 5th Infantry Brigade soldiers march past German civilians from Xanten, the 'gateway to the Rhine'. Along Xanten's outskirts and within the town, the Canadian 2nd division's 4th Infantry Brigade encountered HMG fire from fortified houses. Allied Crocodile tanks and Wasp Universal Carriers were utilised to reduce enemy positions, along with AT guns and PIATs to destroy the remaining Panzer VI (Tiger) tanks of the German 116th Panzer Division. Elements of the 43rd Wessex Division also participated in Xanten's capture. (NARA)

US Ninth Army soldiers inflate lifebelts on the west bank of the Roer River before the crossings of Operation Grenade, which started on 23 March as the flood stage receded. Fifteen east bank German-defended villages and 1,400 POWs were captured on the river crossing's first day. (NARA)

An American engineer attached to the US Ninth Army's 30th Infantry Division ignites smoke pots to conceal the Roer River crossing near Schephoven during Operation Grenade's initial day on 23 March. The wind's unpredictability caused the smoke-screen to blow in the wrong direction, necessitating the movement of the concealment method to other crossing sites. (*USAMHI*)

American 334th IR soldiers from the XIII Corps' 84th Division paddle across the swollen Roer River in their twelve-man steel assault boat near Linnich at the start of US Ninth Army's Operation Grenade on 23 February. Many wore inflatable life belts that prevented drowning when some craft were hit by mortar bombs. The roaring river current also tossed the paddled craft about with many landing on the east bank remote from their intended destinations. Other assault boats with outboard engines often failed due to cold weather. (NARA)

American soldiers of the 2nd Battalion, 120th IR of the US Ninth Army's 30th Division cross the Roer River via a wooden duck-board bridge as remnants of a smoke-screen loomed (background) during Operation Grenade on 23 February. (USAMHI)

(**Above**) US Ninth Army's 84th Infantry Division's soldiers take cover behind a hummock with their 0.30-inch calibre LMG near Linnich, on the eastern side of the Roer River, on 23 February. After the initial elements of the 334th IR's 1st Battalion paddled across the river in steel assault boats, subsequent waves came under German mortar and MG fire. (NARA)

(**Opposite, above**) US Ninth Army's 30th Infantry Division troops take cover on the west bank of the Roer River from Nazi MG fire across the waterway. These infantrymen were preparing to cross the swollen river on 23 February. The inflatable life-vests can be seen on the soldiers' waists as they were lying prone with very little cover. (NARA)

(**Opposite, below**) US combat engineers atop a 2nd Armoured Division M4 medium tank as it crosses a pontoon boat treadway bridge built soon after the successful Roer River crossing during Operation Grenade in late February. After crossing the river, Simpson's forces were to drive northward to meet with the Canadian First Army's British XXX Corps at Geldern as the latter formation moved south along the Niers River from Goch and Weeze. (NARA)

(**Opposite, above**) US Ninth Army's 5th Armoured Division's M4 medium tanks as part of Gillem's XIII Corps duel with German entrenched positions on the east bank of the Roer River as Simpson attempts a link-up with the Canadian First Army. The American tankers were combating the German 338th Infantry Division near Erklenz, which was situated on a plain deemed perfect for armoured advance. (*NARA*)

(**Opposite, below**) German POWs after their capture by US 2nd Battalion soldiers of the 30th Division's 120th IR, XIX Corps near Krauthausen on 23 February, the start date of the US Ninth Army's Operation Grenade, which successfully crossed the receding flooded Rohr River at Julich. Hastily assembled *Volksgrenadier* battalions often ran away from the American advance. Typically, these German units were older and less battle-worthy than the SS Panzergrenadiers and the *Luftwaffe's* parachute formations combating the Canadian First Army's divisions to the north during Operation Veritable. (*USAMHI*)

(**Above**) An American machine-gunner atop his armoured vehicle, alert for German aircraft, on a street in Remagen after elements of Major-General John Milliken's III Corps' 9th Armoured Division, the latter under the command of Major-General John Leonard, crossed the Ludendorff Railway Bridge on 7 March. The bridgehead expansion followed against elements of the German LXVIII Corps along the elevated terrain of the Erpeler Ley and within the town of Erpel on the east bank of the Rhine River. (*USAMHI*)

(**Opposite, above**) Brigadier-General William Hoge's CCB of the US First Army's 9th Armoured Division moves troops and vehicles across the intact Ludendorff Railway Bridge at Remagen soon after German demolitions failed to completely destroy the structure across the Rhine River. The mostly intact railway bridge's twin stone towers on the eastern side of the bridge are visible (*background*). These troops and M4 medium tanks were deployed to strengthen the First Army's bridgehead against Nazi armoured counter-attacks, along with numerous *Luftwaffe* sorties to destroy the Ludendorff Bridge and other temporary bridges erected across the Rhine River. (*USAMHI*)

(**Above**) A sign that appeared on one of the Ludendorff Railway Bridge's stone towers reads: 'CROSS THE RHINE WITH DRY FEET COURTESY OF THE 9th ARMD DIV'. In addition to maintaining the intact span of the bridge, the first of several tactical treadway bridges was built nearby by the 291st Engineer Combat Battalion on 11 May. (*USAMHI*)

(**Opposite, below**) American engineers lay wooden planking on a Bailey bridge section of the Ludendorff Railway Bridge, which was destroyed by the detonation of German demolitions under the eastern pier. This section was further damaged when an American TD slipped in the cratered section of the bridge soon after it had been captured on 7 March by a charge from Company A, 27th Armoured Infantry Battalion, led by Lieutenant Karl Timmerman. (*USAMHI*)

(**Above**) US First Army infantrymen from 1st Division's 16th IR (veterans of Omaha Beach at Normandy) take cover in a doorway and behind a disabled Nazi Panzer V (Panther) tank on a street in Bonn on 9 March 1945. GFM Model predicted that American forces would concentrate on the Rhine near Bonn as the country farther upriver would be more difficult for them to progress. Model's subordinate, German Fifteenth Army commander von Zangen, who was resisting US Ninth Army's movement across the Rhineland after the Roer River crossings, argued that the real danger for an American breakthrough to the Rhine was south-east of the Ahr River at Remagen, where US First Army's III Corps, under General Milliken, was moving. Remagen was not to be reinforced by Model in compliance with Hitler's directive to abandon West Wall defences to provide reinforcements for other sectors. (*NARA*)

(**Opposite, above**) US Third Army infantrymen of the XX Corps' 94th Division run across an open area between ruined buildings in the town of Sinz located on the Moselle River near Trier in the Saar region, on 8 February. Patton's forces had crossed the Our River and the Siegfried Line to arrive at this point. (*NARA*)

(**Opposite, below**) A US Third Army's 87th Infantry Division's LMG position amid the ruins of Coblenz as a supporting M4 medium tank moves through the debris-strewn street. Coblenz was south of the recently acquired Remagen bridgehead at the junction of the Moselle and Rhine Rivers. Patton had indicated to Eisenhower and Bradley that the West Wall defences in the Saar region could be outflanked and his armour could then start the 'Rhine Rat Race' and drive into the rear of the German First Army. On 13 March, Patton unleashed two of his corps, the XX and XII, across the Moselle for a rapid advance into the Saar-Palatinate region. The Germans then began a limited tactical withdrawal under a veiled suggestion by the new C-in-C West, GFM Kesselring. (*NARA*)

(**Above**) A trio of US Third Army infantrymen cover a street in the Saar-Palatinate region on 20 March. In the two weeks of combat in this sector during the Third Army's approach to the Rhine River, the *Wehrmacht* suffered more than 175,000 casualties and prisoners captured. On this day, the German Seventh Army was given permission to retreat eastwards across the Rhine River while surviving units of the German First Army held the last three remaining bridges, which were soon to be destroyed. (*NARA*)

(**Opposite, above**) After the successful Roer River crossing of late February during Operation Grenade, an infantry column from the US Ninth Army's 35th Infantry Division passes a disabled M24 Chaffee light tank on the road to Rheinberg situated between Alpen to the north and Moers to the south, along the west bank of the Rhine River on 6 March. The M24 Chaffee light tank entered full service with the US Army in late 1944 and had a 75mm main turret gun. (*NARA*)

(**Opposite, below**) US Ninth Army's 35th Division infantrymen crouch at the roadside, taking cover from German mortar and MG fire during the advance to the Rhine River near Kamp Linfort south of Alpen and north-west of Moers on 6 March. (*NARA*)

A US Ninth Army observer watches enemy activity with his binoculars along the east bank of the Rhine River from a ruined building's entranceway. Simpson's XVI and XIII Corps were situated along the west bank of the river across from the southern end of Wesel to Duisburg. (*NARA*)

Chapter Five

Rhine River Crossings and Airborne Assault (23–24 March 1945)

Montgomery's set-piece battle plan

The 21st AG's Rhine River assault was principally aimed at capturing Wesel's road network and then fanning out across the waterway's east bank. The Canadian First Army held the hard-won northern Rhineland sector between the Rhine and Maas Rivers from Emmerich to Nijmegen after Operations Veritable and Blockbuster, and was to move northwards to trap Nazi forces still present in Holland. The British Second Army was tasked with a set piece Rhine crossing between Rees and Wesel opposite Xanten on the west bank. Dempsey's Second Army, comprising British XXX and XII Corps on the left and right respectively, was to utilise battle-hardened units for the river assault. After successful crossings of the Rhine, the British Second Army was to drive north-east towards the German plain.

The 9th Infantry Brigade of the Canadian 3rd Division was attached to the British 51st Highland Division for the launch of their initial river crossing at Rees at 2100 hours on 23 March. The Scottish 15th Division was to attack across the Rhine River from Xanten onto Bislich at 0200 hours on 24 March. The British 1st Commando Brigade was to spearhead the river assault against the vital locale of Wesel during Operation Widgeon, following a more than 1,000-ton HE RAF bombing raid on that locale. At 2200 hours on 23 March, the commandos were to paddle across the water to 2 miles west of Wesel and then move quietly towards this important road centre objective. Wesel was to be transformed into a mass of rubble. However, the German defenders were to stubbornly hold on to their positions amid the ruins.

Simpson's US Ninth Army was to cross the Rhine with its XVI Corps' 30th and 79th Infantry Divisions near Rheinberg. During the daylight of 24 March, Ridgeway's XVIII Airborne Corps, comprising the US 17th and British 6th Airborne Divisions, were to land via parachute drop and glider landings (Operation Varsity), 1–2 miles east of the Rhine to disrupt Wesel's defences, hinder any German troop movements west towards the river, and to expand the bridgehead.

NETH.
GER.

Emmerich

Isselburg

xx ⊠ 15

xxx ▭ XLVII

Bocholt

Aa

FIRST Para

xx ▭ 116

II Can

Rhine

Kalflach

Speldrop

xx ⊠ 6

Wertherbruch

xxx ⊠ II

Issel

Dingden

Rees

xx ⊠ 8

To Cleve 2.7 mi.

Calcar

xx ⊠ 51 Br

Haffen

xx ⊠ 7

xxx ⊠ XVIII

Ringenberg

Hamminkeln

Brunen

LXXXVI xxx ⊠

xxx ⊠ XXX Br

xx ⊠ 6 Br

Airborne Drop Zone

xx ⊠ 17

To Goch 1.9 mi.

Niers

Udem

Hoch-wald

Br. SECOND xxxx
(Dempsey)

Balberger-wald

xx ⊠ 15 Br

Xanten

Bislich

xx ⊠ 84

Rhine

Wesel

Lippe

Weeze

Kervenheim

xxx ⊠ XII Br

Sonsbeck

x ⊠ 1 Cmdo Br

xx ⊠ 30

xx ⊠ 180

Voerde

Kevelaer

Alpen

xxx ⊠ XVI

Rheinberg

xx ⊠ 79

Dinslaken

xx ⊠ Hamburg

VIIII Br xxx ⊠

Walsum

LXIII xxx ⊠

Geldern

Kamp Lintfort

Rhine

NINTH xxxx
(Simpson)

xxx ⊠ XIII

Moers

Homberg

xx ⊠ 2

Duisburg

Straelen

xxx ⊠ XIX

Aldekerk

Rheinhausen

GER.
NETH.

0   5 miles

⬜ US forces	xxxxx Army Group	xx Division	⊠ Infantry	⊠ Airborne Infantry
⬛ Allied forces	xxxx Army	x Brigade		
⬛ German forces	xxx Corps		▭ Armour	➔ US and Allied
			⊠ Panzer-grenadier	bridgeheads and advances

The east bank of the Rhine River was criss-crossed by a sophisticated trench system with interconnecting communication works that enabled German defenders to move forward or retreat without detection. Concertina wire lay in front of the trenches followed by large swaths of acreage with sown mines. Behind the minefields, all domestic or commercial structures were housing sites for concealed 88mm guns, machine-guns and infantry. Further to the rear, the Germans had heavy guns to bombard an Allied beachhead on the east bank of the river.

Opposing the British 21st Army Group's crossing of the Rhine River was Blaskowitz's AG H. The German First Parachute Army, with its II Parachute and XLVII Panzer Corps, was situated between Wesel and Emmerich. The German 6th, 7th and 8th Parachute Divisions of Meindl's II Parachute Corps were to bear the brunt of the initial Allied crossings while von Luttwitz's XLVII Panzer Corps (116th Panzer and 15th Panzergrenadier Divisions) was in reserve 15 miles north-east of Emmerich on the eastern side of the Issel River. Their disposition in the rear had irritated Kesselring. However, Blaskowitz argued that he kept the Panzer formations as reserves to break-up any Allied landings on the east bank before bridgeheads could be established with the crossing of heavy weapons. Kesselring finally concurred with Blaskowitz's strategy to have his Panzers ready in the rear to thwart any major British 21st AG breakthrough.

Montgomery's 21st AG Rhine River crossing. After the 3,000-gun 21st AG artillery bombardment of the eastern shore of the Rhine River during the evening hours of 23 March began, the waterway's assaults commenced during the overnight of 23–24 March. To the north, units of the British 51st Highland Division crossed the river to attack Rees and Speldrop to start Operation Plunder. Operation Widgeon involved the British 1st Commando Brigade assault on Wesel, which was later reinforced with the 1st Cheshire Regiment. The 15th Scottish Division crossed the Rhine in the vicinity of Xanten to attack Bislich and Haffen, among other sites. Confronting Montgomery's orchestrated assaults were the German First Parachute Army's 6th, 7th and 8th Parachute and the 84th Infantry Divisions. In Blaskowitz's AG H reserve was the German XLVII Panzer Corps situated to the east of the Issel River. Later on 24 March, Operation Varsity commenced as an air armada of USAAF and RAF Douglas C-47 twin-engined Skytrain/Dakota and C-46 Commando transports, along with four-engined British Short Stirlings and Handley Page Halifax bombers ferried the paratroopers and towed the Waco, Horsa and Hamilcar gliders of the US XVIII Airborne Corps, comprising the US 17th and British 6th Airborne Divisions, to landing fields on the eastern bank of the Rhine River near Hamminkeln and Ringenberg north of Wesel, in an attempt to disrupt the westward movement of German reinforcements on the Issel River bridges. To the south, Simpson's Ninth Army's XVI Corps' veteran 30th and 79th Infantry crossed the Rhine River to the east of Alpen and Rheinberg to assault the *Wehrmacht*'s 180th Infantry Division's defences near Voerde and Dinslaken, as well as the Hamburg Division in the vicinity of Walsum, after a preceding artillery bombardment that commenced at 0100 hours on 24 March. (*Meridian Mapping*)

The Rhine River crossings
Operation Plunder

An enormous Allied artillery bombardment commenced at 1800 hours on 23 March. Three hours later, the first assault wave of the British 51st Highland Division began the river crossing between Rees and Speldrop, to the north-west of Xanten, in storm boats, LVTs (Buffaloes), DUKWs and later ferries. This first wave included the 1st and 7th Black Watch, the 7th Argyll and Sutherland, and the 5/7th Gordon Highlanders, who crossed the waterway in six minutes with the assistance of Buffaloes of the 4th RTR and the Northamptonshire Yeomanry. Enemy return fire was deemed negligible, but the assault force began to incur German resistance from elements of the *Luftwaffe's* 6th and 8th Parachute Divisions (of II Parachute Corps) less than 2 miles inland near Speldrop. The downstream north-westward advance along the east bank towards Emmerich was hindered by this mounting tenacious German defence.

The arrival of British tanks reinforced the 51st Highland Division's movement along the east bank. The capture of Rees was assigned to a battalion of the Gordon Highlanders, who were to assist the Canadian 3rd Division's 9th Infantry Brigade's river assault north-west towards Emmerich. However, stiff resistance by Meindl's II Parachute Corps persisted during the later morning hours of 24 March to the north of Speldrop necessitated reinforcements with the 2nd Seaforth Highlanders, who crossed the Rhine River in storm boats and passed through a Black Watch unit to sever the roads, enabling additional Nazi reinforcements. Fierce fighting in the vicinity of Emmerich continued for the next several days.

Operation Widgeon

Opposite Wesel, Operation Widgeon commenced one hour (2200 hours 23 March) after the 51st Highland Division's crossing. The 1st Commando Brigade, under British Second Army's XII Corps (Ritchie) command, comprising the No. 3 and No. 6 British Commandos and the No. 45 and 46 RM Commandos. No. 6 Commandos, assisted by RE's 84th Field Company, crossed the 400-yard-wide watery expanse in their storm boats, making noise with their outboard motors. Nazi shelling of this crossing with mortars and artillery was extremely accurate with many storm boats hit and commando casualties. No. 6 Commandos stormed into enemy trenches in darkness, incurring more casualties. However, the outskirts of Wesel were reached by 2230 hours. Then, the RAF's heavy bombers pounded Wesel in a massive fifteen-minute aerial attack, which levelled the urban and communications centre. The mounds of rubble created were to provide the Nazi defenders, comprising battle-hardened parachute troops as well as less battle-worthy *Volkssturm* battalions, with numerous defensive positions from which to stage a tenacious fight.

No. 46 RM Commandos and the brigade's tactical HQ crossed in Buffaloes of the RE's 77th Assault Squadron and assaulted Wesel by landing at Grav Insel on the

Rhine's east bank. No. 45 RM Commandos and No. 3 Commandos soon followed in later waves of Buffaloes.

Although von Luttwitz wanted to immediately deploy his XLVIII Panzer Corps tanks to Wesel coincident with the commandos' crossings, Kesselring was wary of an upcoming airborne assault and held off on this counter-attack. However, by 0900 hours on 24 March, orders were given that Wesel was to be re-taken from the commando assault force. Panzergrenadiers, with Mk IV Panzers and SPGs, moved onto the commando positions in piecemeal attacks that were often prematurely halted in response to the commandos' light infantry weapons of MGs and PIATs. Nonetheless, the commando crossing at Wesel was a contentious bridgehead. Then, as the morning combat continued, thousands of Allied aircraft appeared overhead for the start of Operation Varsity. It was not until dawn of 25 March that the commandos, with the assistance of the British 1st Cheshire Regiment, which also crossed the Rhine in Buffaloes, announced the end of all German resistance in Wesel.

Crossing of the 15th Scottish Division at Xanten

At 0100 hours on 24 March, another enormous preparatory artillery bombard-ment commenced. From near Xanten soon thereafter, two battalions from the 15th Scottish Division's 44th Lowland Brigade crossed the Rhine in Buffaloes north-west of Wesel in the British XII Corps' zone against light German machine-gun opposition initially at the river bank, and then more inland at crossroads and farmhouses by elements of the German 7th Parachute and 84th Infantry Divisions, the latter unit belonging to Straube's LXXXVI Corps. In three waves, spaced four minutes apart, the 8th Royal Scots Battalion crossed. The 15th Scottish Division's other leading 227th Brigade crossed the Rhine in Buffaloes of the East Riding Yeomanry. Also, at 2300 hours on 23 March, the 10th Highland Light Infantry and 2nd Argyll and Sutherland Highlanders crossed the 300-yard river width in Buffaloes. They encountered stiff resistance by the German defenders. It was not until 0630 hours on 24 March that the division's 46th Brigade's 7th Seaforth Highlanders passed through the initial assault force to seize important east bank objectives.

Later on 24 March, the 43rd Wessex and 53rd Welsh crossed the great river and drove inland to the east. Twenty-first AG's 7th, 11th and the Guards Armoured Divisions were poised along the west bank of the river for their crossing to drive towards the northern Ruhr industrial region and beyond. Also, the Canadian 2nd and remainder of the Canadian 3rd Infantry Divisions soon crossed the waterway. These latter forces were to join the Canadian 9th Brigade, attached to the 51st Highland Division, to commence a drive up the river's east bank into northern Holland.

US Ninth Army crossing

Following a massive artillery bombardment (65,000 shells fired in one hour), com-mencing at 0100 hours on 24 March, and aerial sorties (1,500 bombers) against

German airfields, the US Ninth Army's XVI Corps initially sent the 30th Division's three infantry regiments across an 8-mile front spanning from Büderich, Wallach and Rheinberg, beginning at 0200 hours, utilising a smoke-screen. The leading 30th Division unit was comprised of three battalions of the US 119th Infantry Regiment. These infantrymen manhandled their heavy assault boats over a dyke before immersing them into the Rhine's waters. Then the soldiers started the outboard motors and began crossing the river. Minutes later, the assault boats reached the east bank and the troops splashed ashore, each unit abreast of one another.

At 0300 hours, the 313th and 315th Infantry Regiments of Ninth Army's 79th Division began their crossing of the Rhine at Rheinberg, south of the Lippe River, in storm boats. US combat engineers were plentiful to expedite a far bank build-up and assist with the storm boats' crossings.

The American crossing was opposed by two corps of the First Parachute Army: the LXXXVI holding Wesel and the river from the Lippe River to Dinslaken, and the LVIII situated below Duisburg. In the LXXXVI sector, units of the German 180th Infantry Division were stunned by both the bombardment and suddenness of the assault. Virtually no active defence was mounted against the American crossing and only a few dozen US Ninth Army casualties were incurred. By the morning of 24 March, eight infantry battalions of the US 30th Division and five of the 79th were across the Rhine River.

Operation Varsity

For Montgomery's airborne assault, the First Allied Airborne Army employed Lieutenant-General Matthew Ridgway's US XVIII Airborne Corps (under Dempsey's British Second Army tactical control) with General Richard Gale, his British deputy. Gale had previously led the British 6th Airborne's parachute and glider landings during the Normandy assault. The US XVIII Airborne Corps comprised the US 17th Airborne and the British 6th Airborne Divisions, under the command of Major-General William Miley and Major-General E.L. Bois respectively. The US 17th Airborne was reorganised and equipped after infantry combat during the Ardennes campaign.

Ridgway parachute-dropped and air-landed his two XVIII Corps divisions in one enormous rapid lift onto a confined landing zone amid the high ground in the vicinity of the Diersfordterwald, between the Rhine and Issel Rivers. Tactically, this was to prevent another Arnhem fiasco where troops once on the ground had to make lengthy marches from their drop-zones to their destinations. The XVIII Airborne's objectives were just to the east of thickly-wooded Diersfordterwald. There, they were to seize and occupy road junctions at Hamminkeln, and the Issel River bridges. Possession of these bridges and the canal was to prevent von Luttwitz's XLVII Corps' tanks of the 116th Panzer Division from reaching the bridgeheads across the Rhine River. The Allied airborne forces, by controlling the approaches to the Rhine from the east, would create a protected zone from Wesel to the Issel River into which British Second Army's XII Corps was to attack. Elements of the German 7th Parachute and 84th Infantry Divisions were defending the area of the airborne assault.

At 1000 hours on 24 March, 900 Allied Typhoon and Thunderbolt fighter-bombers escorted 1,700 paratroop-carrying C-47 Dakota transports, which also towed many of the 2,000-plus gliders. The total strength was 21,600 airborne infantrymen for the operation's parachute drop and air landing to the north-east of Wesel. British 6th Airborne troops were flown from airfields in England while their American counterparts in the 17th Airborne Division came from twelve airfields in the vicinity of Paris. Over Belgium, both of the XVIII Corps' airborne divisions made a rendezvous for the final leg to the drop-zone across the Rhine. The magnitude of Operation Varsity eclipsed both the Normandy and Arnhem airborne operations.

Major-General Paul Williams, leader of IX Troop Carrier Command, planned to fly the paratroopers' transports abreast of one another to shorten a parachute brigade's drop-time to two minutes instead of the customary ten. The gliders followed the paratroopers' drop to deliver the glider infantry as well as the support and HQ echelons of the two airborne divisions. As the gliders followed the parachute drop, the element of surprise was lost and Nazi flak ground-fire exacted a steep price on the slowly descending aircraft onto their landing zones.

The 1st Canadian Parachute Battalion, under Lieutenant-Colonel J.S. Nicklin, was attached to the British 6th Airborne's 3rd Parachute Brigade. It was charged with the clearance, after securing its drop-zone, of the wooded area atop the Schneppenburg feature. Many Canadians, including Nicklin, were killed by German MG fire before they could get out of their parachute harnesses, or they died after falling onto nearby trees. But a sufficient force of Canadian paratroopers amassed to fend off the Nazi defenders as well as a Panzer counter-attack.

The initial American paratrooper drop, flying lower than the British 6th Airborne one, comprised the 507th RCT. Its 'sticks' reached ground more safely from enemy fire north-east of Wesel near the Diersfordt Castle. However, the C-47 Dakota transports were exposed to more accurate German flak and losses were high. After amassing troops and removing heavier weapons from air-dropped canisters, Colonel Raff moved his 507th PIR forces to clear the woods of German MGs and heavier ordnance. Colonel James Coutt's 515th PIR reached their objective and found that 'Raff's Ruffians' had already cleared it of any enemy. The 515th PIR then came under 20mm and 88mm Nazi gunfire.

Elements of the British 6th Airborne followed the American parachute drop and suffered many mid-air casualties from Nazi gunfire tearing into the paratroopers' 'chutes. The British 6th Air-Landing Brigade arrived after the parachute battalions were already on the ground. The 12th Devons were assigned to take Hamminkeln, which was defended by Germans behind a screen of light flak guns manned by elements from a *Luftwaffe* Regiment, some *Volkssturm*, and parachute divisions that were bolstering the German 84th Infantry Division. Isolated German pockets of resistance and local counter-attacks were present in various places across the landing zones between Wesel and the Issel River. The 2nd Oxfordshire and Buckinghamshire Light Infantry were tasked with the seizure of the railway bridges between Hamminkeln and Ringenberg. The 1st Royal Ulster Rifles were to attempt the capture of an intact Issel River bridge.

Although Varsity surprised the Germans, the 116th Panzer Division, with several Mk IV tanks, counter-attacked the US 194th Glider Infantry Regiment, which was tasked with the seizure of the Issel River bridges. The glidermen used their 'bazookas' to good effect, disabling a number of Panzers at a range of 100 yards.

More than 200 B-24 Liberators followed with almost 600 tons of supplies dropped to the airborne assault troops below within two hours of landing. An extensive Allied fighter umbrella remained over the battlefield to interdict *Luftwaffe* sorties and to provide ground-support attacks, while a tactical bomber force was dispatched to neutralise local Nazi airfields, marshalling yards and assorted military targets that could be implemented against Varsity.

Several C-47s and gliders were hit by flak, resulting in ground crashes and many casualties. The British Airlanding units' glidermen were assailed by flak and those who landed successfully were met by German machine-gunfire. Combat ensued in close proximity to their glider craft, many wrecked. By nightfall of Varsity's initial day, fierce combat eliminated the German 84th Division's defenders and artillery. Then the Allied airborne troops effected a link-up with the main force crossing the Rhine River as British armour would be needed to help fend-off counter-attacks by the German 116th Panzer Division heading across the Issel River from the east after it was committed to battle by von Luttwitz, the Nazi XLVII Corps commander. The 116th Panzer Division dispatched several tanks towards the paratroopers and glidermen with the intention of crossing the Issel River bridges. However, the 17-pounders, which had remained functional after the glider landings, were deployed against the Panzers and sent them reeling. Additional German counter-attacks were beginning to take their toll on the 6th Airlanding Brigade's 2nd Oxfordshire and Buckingham Light Infantry forces. Elements of the 12th Devonshire Regiment were sent to reinforce their fellow glidermen, but determined Panzer thrusts towards the Issel River road bridge compelled the Oxford and Bucks' leader to demolish the bridge during the night of 24–25 March. By 27 March, the British had crossed the Issel and Lippe Rivers on the north side of the Ruhr Region.

On 25 March, tough combat was encountered by elements of the British Second Army fighting units of the German 7th Parachute and General Rott's 15th Panzergrenadier Divisions beyond Rees along the road to Emmerich to the north-west. Every house had to be cleared by Wasp flame-throwers, followed by infantrymen clearing enemy cellar redoubts. Further to the east, a 17-mile salient was created by American paratroopers atop the British 6th Guards Armoured Tank Brigade's Churchill tanks. On 28 March, Montgomery announced that the battle to cross Germany's great boundary river had been won. He unleashed his six armoured divisions, numbering over a thousand tanks for 21st AG's drive towards the northern portion of the Ruhr industrial sector.

Montgomery's use of a huge and elaborate Rhine River crossing enabled him to have a massive force available for his armoured thrust onto the north German plain. By utilising several crossing points and Operation Varsity's airborne operation, Montgomery confused the Nazi defenders as to the exact location of the river assault while, in fact, he was to secure a number of different bridgeheads. When the Nazis committed their Panzers for a counter-attack, Allied airborne forces had already seized the vital Issel River bridges to block their advance towards the east bank bridgeheads.

US Third and Seventh Armies' Rhine River crossings

After the *coup de main* US 5th Division crossings at Oppenheim and Nierstein, Patton's forces assaulted the Rhine before daylight on 25 March at Boppard, which was situated to the north of the confluence of the Rhine and Main Rivers. This latter crossing by the US 87th Infantry Division was fiercely resisted by von Zangen, with reinforcements from Felber's Seventh Army. Also, late on 27 March, Patton sent Walker's XX Corps' 80th Division across the Rhine in another amphibious assault between his VIII and XII Corps at Mainz. The 80th Division's infantrymen had no difficulty in this crossing. By day's end, Wiesbaden was captured with extremely light casualties. Patton's three corps were instructed to move on Giessen and link-up with the US First Army moving south from their Remagen bridgehead.

Lieutenant-General Patch's Seventh Army reached the west bank of the Rhine a week after its drive through the Saar-Palatinate. On 23 March, the US Seventh Army's XV Corps took over the river bank from Third Army troops and prepared to cross the Rhine with reserve regiments of the battle-hardened US 3rd and 45th Infantry Divisions. The crossing at Worms was made by the 3rd Division's 15th and 30th IRs against light opposition, while the 45th Division crossed between Hamm and the Rheim-Durkheim area. An originally planned airborne operation was delayed and the crossing commenced without it at 0230 hours on 26 March by two IRs in storm boats. The defenders were the remnants of many shattered German divisions. Heavy Allied artillery fire ensued when the element of surprise evaporated. Although the river's 1,000-foot width was crossed by the 45th Division's 179th and 180th IRs in under a minute, the Germans countered with heavy mortar- and gunfire, which scored numerous hits on the storm boats causing many soldiers to drown, particularly in the second assault wave. US combat engineers from the 40th and 540th Engineer

Combat Groups erected bridges enabling a thousand vehicles to cross the Rhine, including tanks and TDs, within the initial twenty-four hours of the assault.

By the night of 26 March, the assaulting elements of the US Seventh Army linked-up with Patton's Third Army and the American forces moved 8 miles inland from the Rhine's east bank to cross the Darmstadt-Mannheim autobahn. The Germans did not regard this area with any strategic importance. Thus, by 27 March, the enemy defenders retreated. The German forces in General Felber's Seventh Army comprised mostly old men of the *Volkssturm*, with a few regular *Wehrmacht* infantry battalions. After their defence crumbled, Hitler sacked Felber and replaced him with General Hans von Obstfelder.

First French Army Rhine River crossings

To secure a foothold on German soil after strong urging by General Charles de Gaulle, president of the Provisional Government of France, the 3rd Algerian Division crossed with small forces at Speyer at 0330 hours on 31 March. In de Gaulle's view, this would enable the French to gain a zone of occupation in post-war Germany. This was followed by elements of the 2nd Moroccan Division crossing upstream against enemy fire at Germersheim. A third French Rhine crossing was made at Leimersheim, between Germersheim and Karlsruhe, on 2 April, to speed up the capture of that latter locale. A final fourth crossing was made at Strasbourg on 6 April, as the campaign entered a new phase. Then, the French forces began their drive on Stuttgart.

A 21st AG 5.5-inch calibre medium gun erupts at the commencement of the artillery barrage at 2200 hours on 23 March. The magnitude of the preparatory bombardment before the actual Rhine River crossings hours later amounted to 3,300 guns. (*NARA*)

(**Above**) An RA heavy 7.2-inch calibre Howitzer crew loads the weapon's breech at the start of Operation Plunder. At 2200 hours on 23 March, the gunners opened up their massive barrage on German positions on the Rhine River's east bank. Assisting the 1st Commando Brigade's Operation Widgeon were the numerous batteries of British XII Corps artillery, including 40mm Bofors AA firing orange-coloured tracer rounds, 25-pounder field cannon and the 5.5-inch guns of the RA's medium regiments. (*NARA*)

(**Opposite, above**) British troops in leather jerkins carry their assault boat through a wooded area towards the western bank of the Rhine River for Operation Plunder's crossings to start. The lead river assaults were made by the 51st Highland and the 15th Scottish Divisions as well as 1st Commando Brigade (Operation Widgeon). To the south, the US Ninth Army's 30th and 79th Infantry Divisions made the initial American crossings to the east bank of the river. (*NARA*)

(**Opposite, below**) A line of American tank transporters carry USN LCVPs through a Belgian town from the port of Antwerp to the west bank of the Rhine River. These LCVPs fulfilled many roles in addition to ferrying infantry troops, tanks and vehicles across the Rhine River. (*USN*)

(**Above**) A patrol of the British No. 6 Commandos hunt snipers and hidden German troops in the ruins of Wesel on 24 March during Operation Widgeon after crossing the Rhine River the night before in storm boats assisted by the RE's 84th Field Company. After the river crossing, which commenced at 2200 hours on 23 March, No. 6 Commandos advanced along the river bank and were at Wesel's outskirts thirty minutes later. During one search of a ruined building's cellar, Wesel's German Garrison commander was killed after refusing to surrender, and a map of the area's flak positions was found, which was to prove important for the upcoming Operation Varsity. (*Author's Collection*)

(**Opposite, above**) Infantrymen from the 1st Battalion, Cheshire Regiment disembark LVTs (Buffaloes) after crossing the Rhine River in support of the 1st Commando Brigade's assault on Wesel on 24 March. The destroyed Wesel railway bridge has collapsed in the river (*background*) after being demolished earlier in the month. (*NARA*)

(**Opposite, below**) British infantrymen from the 43rd Wessex Division's 5th Battalion, Dorsetshire Regiment disembark LVTs (Buffaloes) of the 4th RTR and the Northamptonshire Yeomanry on the Rhine River's east bank after crossing on 25 March to support the previous assault by elements of the 51st Highland Division's 153rd and 154th Brigades on 23–24 March. The 1st Gordons of the 51st Highland Division were tasked with clearing the Rhine River town of Rees between Emmerich and Wesel. The 5th Dorsetshire crossed the river and took the villages of Speldrop and Androp against light opposition, while the 4th Dorsetshire captured Millingen. (*NARA*)

(**Above**) A mobile triple-mounted Polsten (a simpler version of the original Oerlikon design) AA gun atop an armoured vehicle (probably a Crusader tank) within a sand-bagged, hessian-camouflaged gun-pit on the eastern bank of the Rhine River. This AA gun-crew was ready to interdict *Luftwaffe* sorties against the waterway's crossing sites on 25 March. (*Author's Collection*)

(**Opposite, above**) Almost a score of RAF Hawker Tempest Mk Vs of the Allied 2nd TAF fly at 10,000 feet after attacking enemy trains and motorised columns on the eastern side of the Rhine River. With four 20mm cannon in the leading edges of the wings as well as up to a 2,000 bomb external bomb- and/or rocket-load carried under the wings, these formidable fighter-bombers wreaked havoc on reinforcing German LXXXVI units moving westward towards the Issel River to contest the 21st AG's crossings and US XVIII Airborne's Corps parachute and air landing glider assaults. (*NARA*)

(**Opposite, below**) A British reconnaissance section with their signal devices ascends an area of the Rhine's eastern riverbank on 24 March. Initial opposition to the 21st AG's crossings was light. However, the usual German counter-attack on Wesel ensued by elements of the First Parachute Army with Panzers units. (*NARA*)

(**Opposite, above**) A British infantry column moves east in single-file past an LVT (Buffalo) on 24 March. By the early hours of this day, the British river assaults were across the Rhine and had consolidated with preparations made to break-out of the bridgehead. The massive 21st AG overnight artillery bombardment had pummelled German defensive positions, especially at Wesel. (*NARA*)

(**Opposite, below**) USN-crewed LCVPs and LVTs ferry troops and ordnance across the Rhine River as part of the US Ninth Army's XVI Corps' 30th and 79th divisional assaults from the south of Wesel to Duisburg. Following-up on the initial assault were to be the 35th and 75th divisional crossings along with that of the 8th Armoured Division, the latter a relatively new formation to the ETO. (*NARA*)

(**Above**) Infantrymen of an assault battalion of US Ninth Army's 119th IR from the 30th Division disembark a steel 55hp motor-powered assault boat onto the east bank of the Rhine River on 24 March. Although later waves were to use LVTs for the river crossing, the slower and noisier assault boats were utilised during the first overnight attack that commenced at 0200 hours. The disembarkation was just south-east of Buderich, a village near the confluence of the Rhine and Lippe Rivers. In all, the US XVI Corps had over 120,000 men with more than fifty artillery battalions to provide bombardment and fire mission support from the west bank of the river. (*NARA*)

Infantrymen from the US Ninth Army's XIV Corps' 30th Division pinned down by Nazi MG fire on the east bank of the Rhine River after the successful crossings. This division was charged with the capture of villages east of the river, including Spellen, Mehrum and Löhnen, which were defended by the *Wehrmacht*'s 180th Division. *(NARA)*

Combat engineers attached to the US Ninth Army assist with the transport of an M4 with a 76mm turret gun on a Bailey Bridge ferry on 24 March. American armour was needed to assist the 30th Division's 119th IR breakthrough of a German roadblock outside Friedrichsfeld. Other M4 medium tanks were needed to aid the 117th IR breakthrough German defenders at a rail crossing north of Voerde as well as the 120th IR to pass across a rail line on the main road from Dinslaken to Wesel. (*NARA*)

A US Ninth Army motorised column of DUKWs, Jeeps and trucks crosses the Rhine River over a pontoon bridge on 27 March to reinforce the 30th and 79th Divisions' break-out to the north-east towards Münster, west of the Ems River, and to the south to be the northern pincer of the Ruhr region's double envelopment. (*NARA*)

(**Opposite, above**) Infantrymen from the US Seventh Army cross the Rhine under heavy fire as they quickly disembark their assault boats. A number were armed with the semi-automatic M1 carbine rifle, which was shorter than the standard M1 Garand rifle and, therefore, easier to deploy into combat from confined spaces, such as steel assault boats. The M1 carbine fired a 0.30-inch calibre bullet from an external box magazine that carried fifteen or thirty rounds. (*NARA*)

(**Opposite, below**) Infantrymen from the US Third Army's 23rd IR of the 5th Division climb into a DUKW for a subsequent Rhine River crossing at Oppenheim during daylight hours of 23 March, 15 miles south of Mainz. Earlier on the night of 22–23 March, a first assault wave paddled their storm boats against light opposition from elements of the *Wehrmacht's* Seventh Army. Patton had driven his XII Corps commander, Major-General Manton Eddy, to cross the river before Montgomery's forces did. There was a small barge harbour at Oppenheim, suitable for launching steel storm boats, which was undetected by the German defenders on the east bank of the river. By dawn, the 23rd IR had six battalions of infantry on the east bank of the Rhine. (*NARA*)

(**Above**) A USN-crewed LCVP ferries US Third Army troops across the Rhine on 24 March. Patton had accumulated a large number of river assault craft, which included twelve LCVPs under naval personnel that had been rehearsing for the river crossing at Toul in France's Lorraine region near the Moselle River. (*NARA*)

(**Above**) Soldiers of the US Third Army's 89th Infantry Division huddle low in their steel storm boat, which they paddled to cross the Rhine under enemy fire at St Goar on 25–26 March. The infantry, after arriving on the east bank, cleared St Goar by the morning of 27 March. However, they suffered nearly 300 casualties in the crossing. Another VIII Corps unit, the 87th Infantry Division, paddled across the river on 25 March in the vicinity of Rhens, where strong enemy resistance from a reinforcing German corps opened on the storm boats with withering fire that tore the craft and infantrymen apart, necessitating the attacking regiment to abandon its attempt and try farther south at Boppard, situated to the north of the confluence of the Rhine and Main Rivers. The crossing site at Boppard proved less difficult. *(NARA)*

(**Opposite**) US 17th Airborne Division paratroopers of the 513th PIR board a C-46 Commando aircraft at an airfield in France. The C-46 was relatively new and this was the plane's first operational mission. The C-46s flew at approximately 500 feet over the Rhine River and met intensive Nazi AA gunfire. A serious flaw with the Commando was soon discovered that if shrapnel hit one of the plane's wing tanks, the leaking fuel drained along the fuselage. An enemy incendiary shell turned many Commando aircraft into fireballs, with extensive loss of aircraft and paratroopers within the initial thirty minutes of combat during Operation Varsity on 24 March. *(NARA)*

(**Above**) Men of the 513th PIR about to jump from their transport during the start of Operation Varsity on 24 March. By the time the transports were crossing the Rhine, many were ablaze from long-range German AA guns. The 513th PIR commander, Colonel Coutts, had jumped from his burning transport only to land amid enemy small-arms fire. Coutts had seen scores of British paratroopers on the ground as British Horsa gliders were starting to skid across the landing zone. His assumption that the British had landed in an American landing zone was incorrect as Coutts and his paratroopers were 1.5 miles north-west of Hamminkeln in the 6th Airborne's zone. (*NARA*)

(**Opposite**) British 6th Airborne planners hoped that a mass drop would frighten the German defenders and minimise resistance. Although it must have produced awe among the Germans to witness the large-scale precision air-drop by elements of British 6th Airborne, the Nazis focused their air-bursts on the tightly packed parachutes as concussive waves and shrapnel destroyed many 'chutes, sending the paratroopers to their death. The 7th Parachute Battalion of the 5th Brigade suffered heavy casualties before they even landed. (*NARA*)

(**Above**) Two four-engined RAF Short Stirling Mk IV bombers tow their Horsa gliders containing the Air-Landing Brigade troops of the British 6th Airborne during Operation Varsity toward their destination zones east of Wesel on 24 March. The Handley Page Halifax bombers towed both Horsa and the larger Hamilcar gliders, the latter delivering critical 17-pounder AT guns to the landing zones. Almost 200 Stirlings participated in Operation Varsity. (*NARA*)

(**Opposite, above**) A British Horsa glider with thirty British 6th Airborne gliderman aboard skids to an abrupt stop upon landing during Operation Varsity on 24 March. While decelerating and stopping, the glider made an inviting target for German AA and MG fire, which inflicted numerous casualties among the glidermen prior to their dis-embarkation. The three battalions comprising the British 6th Air-Landing Brigade were the 1st Royal Ulster Rifles, the 2nd Oxfordshire and Buckinghamshire Light Infantry, and the 12th Devonshire along with 53rd Worcestershire Yeomanry Air-Landing Light Regiment of RA, 249th Field Company of Airborne RE, and 195th (Air-Landing) Field Ambulance of the RAMC. (*NARA*)

(**Opposite, below**) A British 6th Air-Landing Brigade Jeep and towed light AA gun emerge from a Horsa glider in a field near Ringenberg during Operation Varsity on 24 March. The Jeeps were essential for the rapid deployment of glider infantry to sites, such as the Issel River bridges and town of Hamminkeln, to interfere with German reinforcement moving westward towards the Rhine River crossing areas. (*NARA*)

(**Above**) A British 6th Airborne paratrooper in his characteristic beret leads a German with his Sten SMG into captivity. Another wounded German soldier is lying on the ground (*far right*) with his helmet and rifle near the portal of a ruined brick building during Operation Varsity on 24 March. (*NARA*)

(**Opposite, above**) An American paratrooper from the US 17th Airborne Division lies on the ground cradling his M3 SMG ('Grease Gun') among the wounded and dead of a German motorised detail. A building and aerial antenna are visible (*background*). The M3 SMG was developed to replace the more expensive and intricately designed Thompson SMG, but did not enter service with the US Army until 1944. Army ordnance developers emulated some of the finer features of the British Sten and German MP 40 SMGs. The M3 had a 30-round detachable external box magazine and fired the powerful 0.45-inch calibre ACP bullet from an 8-inch barrel, compared to the Thompson's 10.5-inch barrel. (*NARA*)

(**Opposite, below**) American paratroopers from Colonel Raff's 507th PIR ('Raff's Ruffians') after hitting the ground fired their carbines from kneeling and prone positions. They had dropped over a mile from their intended positions in mainly open fields. (*NARA*)

(**Opposite, above**) US 17th Airborne paratroopers gather their gear and assemble their weapons after landing in a partially wooded drop-zone during Operation Varsity on 24 March. Billowing camouflaged parachutes hang from nearby trees. (*NARA*)

(**Opposite, below**) Colonel Raff, commander of the 507th PIR, assembled his paratroopers nearest to him and led them quickly towards the woods where German MGs and heavier ordnance were shelling the landing zones. The Americans charged the woods, incurring casualties, to silence the German gun positions. (*NARA*)

(**Above**) A dead US 17th Airborne Division paratrooper lies in a farm field while other paratroopers crouch to seek cover from German MG fire during Operation Varsity on 24 March. The 507th PIR was brought in at about 600 feet, which was lower in altitude than the British. This gave the Americans a better chance at surviving the flak and MG fire during their descent. However, the Nazi fire wreaked havoc on the US C-47 transports. (*NARA*)

(**Above**) Several American Waco gliders close to one another in a farm field, fortunately away from the power line towers (*right*). However, other obstacles include horses and cows that graze in an adjacent field. (*NARA*)

(**Opposite, above**) An American gliderman rapidly escapes his smashed Waco glider, with bayonet fixed to his M1 Garand rifle. One gliderman said: 'Before you know it, the ground is racing underneath. You are in a pasture, crashing through a fence, bounding across a gully, clipping a tree with a wingtip.' Also, pitched battles with German defenders occurred at dozens of Allied glider landing fields until the gliders emptied and the infantrymen moved towards their objective, the Issel River bridges. (*NARA*)

(**Opposite, below**) An American gliderman crouches in a ditch next to the fencing of a farmer's field. In the background a Waco glider is relatively intact. German MGs, often situated in farmhouses and outbuildings, made the glidermen start digging for any possible cover. Even Nazi 88mm AA/AT guns were employed at the gliders that had just landed. (*NARA*)

(**Opposite, above**) Two US 17th Airborne Division Waco gliders after landing in a farm field during Operation Varsity on 24 May. In the foreground, two glidermen are seen pushing a Jeep out through the raised nose of the Waco. Not all landings went so smoothly. Some gliders were destroyed in mid-air by German AA. Other rough landings resulted in the death of glidermen and pilots before they could disembark, usually with German guns quickly ranging on every glider that reached the ground. (*NARA*)

(**Opposite, below**) US 17th Airborne Division glidermen take cover behind some Jeeps that were air-landed by the Wacos. The drop-zones for glidermen and paratroopers, in addition to being covered by smoke, were laced with German MG-fire, making it extremely hazardous to even retrieve containers with heavier weapons, ammunition and supplies in the face of enemy resistance. (*NARA*)

(**Above**) US 507th PIR paratroopers direct German captives into an open area near the woods where there was fierce combat. After 'Raff's Ruffians', with determined assaults, overwhelmed the German gun battery, more than 300 enemy infantry and artillerymen were taken prisoner along with a colonel. Fifty Germans were killed in this action. (*NARA*)

(**Above**) A wounded American paratrooper being helped from a farm field as one soldier (*far left*) remains alert for any sudden enemy activity. There were so many casualties among the airborne units that field dressing stations were short of medical supplies, particularly stretchers. Additional supplies were brought in by gliders and by the 200 US Eighth Air Force B-24 Liberators dropping them by parachute. (*NARA*)

(**Opposite, above**) A US 17th Airborne Division aid station amid the Operation Varsity landing zones on 24 March. When a company of the Royal Ulster Rifles' glidermen arrived at their Issel River bridge objectives, they found units from the US 513th PIR had parachuted there by mistake. The Royal Ulster Rifles found the fields covered with dead and wounded American paratroopers who were killed while still aloft or machine-gunned after reaching the ground. (*NARA*)

(**Opposite, below**) Members of the British 6th Air-Landing Brigade with their 6-pounder AT gun at a crossroads blocking point in Hamminkeln trying to hold off an enemy armoured counter-attack. The AT guns, some of them 17-pounders, were air-landed by Horsa and Hamilcar gliders. About 200 glidermen of the 2nd Oxfordshire and Buckinghamshire Light Infantry were holding the road and rail bridges between Hamminkeln and Ringneberg. (*Author's Collection*)

(**Above**) A British motorised column crosses the Rhine in late March over a wooden-planked Bailey Bridge on pontoon boats after the initial assault sites were secured permitting the temporary building of such thoroughfares. This bridge was built to connect the Xanten sector with Wesel on the eastern bank. (*NARA*)

(**Opposite, above**) Paratroopers from the US 513th PIR advance towards Münster, accompanied by tanks of the British 6th Coldstream Guards Armoured Brigade, in late March. On 28 March, after crossing the Rhine over the newly erected temporary bridges, Montgomery's 21st AG's tanks, notably the Guards Armoured, 7th ('Desert Rats') and 11th Armoured Divisions, were unleashed to move deeper into Germany. (*NARA*)

(**Opposite, below**) Two British 6th Airborne paratroopers who were briefly captured by the Germans are with their 'liberators', members of the US 17th Airborne Division's 513th PIR who, along with units of the US Ninth Army and tanks of the British 6th Coldstream Guards Armoured Brigade, were moving towards Münster. (*NARA*)

(**Opposite, above**) American Ninth Army soldiers from the 30th Division's 120th IR pass a destroyed German ambulance on their eastward trek through the Wesel Forest on 26 March. This formation was soon to encounter German Panzer units as the northern envelopment of the Ruhr industrial area was commencing. (*NARA*)

(**Opposite, below**) US Ninth Army infantrymen march in Duisburg on 27 March towards a bridge past disabled trolley cars. Duisburg, a city located east of the Rhine River opposite Homberg, was defended by elements of the German LXIII Corps, notably the *Luftwaffe's* 2nd Parachute Division. (*NARA*)

(**Above**) A British military policeman ('Red Cap') directs traffic of US 17th Airborne Division paratroopers mounted atop a column of 6th Armoured Tank Brigade's Churchill tanks for their advance on locales such as Münster on 28 March. (*NARA*)

(**Opposite, above**) A 15th Scottish Division motorised column with infantrymen marching single-file moves along a cobblestoned street in the German city of Bocholt, a road and rail junction on the Aa River, on 29 March. Bocholt is situated just south of the Dutch frontier in the North Rhine-Westphalia region to the east of the Issel River. Bocholt is directly north of Hamminkeln, Ringenberg and Dingden, where British and American airborne forces fought to prevent German LXXXVI Panzer Corps reinforcements from crossing over the Issel River bridges to disrupt the Rhine River crossings. (*NARA*)

(**Above**) An infantry column of the 2nd Monmouthshire Regiment of the British 53rd Welsh Division in XXX Corps moves cautiously through the recently captured road and rail junction of Bocholt. Montgomery's 21st AG forces, after crossing the Rhine River, vectored to the north-east in order to debouch onto the north German plain, ideal for the Allied armoured superiority. (*NARA*)

(**Opposite, below**) The British 7th Armoured ('Desert Rats') Division mass for their advance 7 miles north-east of Wesel onto Brunen as part of Montgomery's breakout from the Rhine bridgeheads east towards the Ruhr region and the north German plain. (*NARA*)

British infantrymen of the Guards Armoured Division fight at night along the left flank of the Second British Army against the *Luftwaffe*'s 7th Parachute Division amid burning buildings near the town of Berge in Lower Saxony after the breakout onto the north German plain in early April. Just to the north-west, Meindl's II Parachute Corps had been putting up fanatical resistance against the British 51st Highland Division's advance beyond Rees. *(NARA)*

Epilogue

The Rhine River crossings by the Allied armies were accomplished with relatively light casualty figures in comparison to the horrific combat losses from mid-December 1944 to early March 1945. Had the Germans withdrawn from the west bank during these winter months to make a decisive stand on the east bank, and had they conserved their resources instead of expending them in the Ardennes attack, they could have inflicted much greater casualties on the Allied forces crossing the river. The Allied planners, commanders and combatants were fortunate that Hitler gambled so much on the Ardennes winter offensive.

Although Churchill was jubilant at the success of the Allied Rhine River crossings, Montgomery was issued an order by Eisenhower that, once the Ruhr industrial region was sealed off, US Ninth Army was to revert to Bradley's 12th AG. Stalin's Soviets were to capture Berlin, not Montgomery's 21st AG. General Gerow's US 15th Army further augmented Bradley's strength to four American armies. Dever's 6th AG and Montgomery's British-Canadian 21st AG were relegated to protecting the flanks of Bradley's massive 12th AG. Historical observers have contended that, similar to the Normandy battle at Caen, British and Canadian forces hammered the Nazi defenders in the northern Rhineland and across the Rhine River, which ultimately led to a massive US 12th AG breakout again.

Montgomery's 21st AG was diverted to the Baltic and reached Lübeck just ahead of the Soviets. As such, with a nascent 'Cold War' starting to fester, Montgomery's forces did block Stalin's entry into Denmark and Scandinavia.

After the successful Rhine River crossings, more than a month of arduous Allied campaigning ensued within Germany before the Third Reich's capitulation on 8 May 1945. Simpson's US Ninth Army met the Soviets on the Elbe River while a portion of Patton's Third Army moved onto Czechoslovakia, only to be re-called by Eisenhower. Another part of Third Army moved into Bavaria and through the Alps to meet FM Harold Alexander's 15th AG coming through the Brenner Pass from Italy into Austria. Hitler's Third Reich, which was supposed to last a thousand years, was completely defeated in under five years from the Allies' Dunkirk evacuation.

(**Opposite, above**) US Army engineers gaze proudly at a sign for a railway bridge across the Rhine River. It commemorated the sacrifice by members of the 355th Engineer General Service (GS) Regiment. This was one of several of the 1056th Engineer Group's engineer and USN 'Seabee' units that constructed the river bridge at Wesel, which had been hotly contested for by the British 1st Commando Brigade and other Allied units on 24 March. (*NARA*)

(**Opposite, below**) Elements of the British 6th Airborne Division, who had fought valiantly on the landing fields near Hamminkeln and Ringenberg during Operation Varsity on 24 March, are being utilised as lorried light infantry. These airborne troops were moving onto Neustadt and Bissendorf towards Celle, the latter a garrison town in Lower Saxony, about 75 miles south of the German port of Hamburg. Celle surrendered to the British on 10 April, sparing it further destruction. (*NARA*)

(**Above**) Downcast German POWs march in formation into captivity under US Seventh Army military guard near Heilbronn on 13 April. More than 15,000 Germans were captured by Montgomery's 21st AG alone during the northern Rhine crossings. (*NARA*)

(**Opposite, above**) Three members of the British military government attached to the British Second Army travel in a Jeep along a German refugee-packed city street to the east of the Rhine River. This waterway proved an illusion to German sovereignty as the Anglo-American armies fanned out to envelop the Ruhr industrial area as well as move onto the Baltic and North Sea port cities. An enormous number of German refugees were also heading west to avoid the Soviet thrust towards Berlin, which Eisenhower agreed to after the crossing of the Rhine. (*NARA*)

(**Opposite, below**) Canadian infantrymen of the *Maisonneuve* Regiment march single-file past a Dutch windmill through Holten *en route* to Rijssen in Holland on 9 April. This formation saw intense combat along the Scheldt Estuary during the Walcheren Island campaign as part of the Canadian 2nd Division's 5th Infantry Brigade. During the final weeks of the war, this unit campaigned in the Battle of Groningen from 13–16 April, in the northern part of Holland with the North Sea to the north-west, before moving on to German locales along the coast. To their shock, the Canadians encountered a Dutch population that had endured occupation and starvation. (*NARA*)

(**Above**) A Canadian soldier reads a street sign in the Dutch city of Groningen, the largest city in the northern part of the Netherlands and the site of the University of Groningen, at the end of the battle for that locale. The sign also indicated the location of an information centre near the German HQ. The Canadian 2nd Division and supporting armoured units were deployed against an *ad hoc* force of 7,000 German soldiers, *Luftwaffe* AA gun-crews as well as Dutch and Belgian SS forces during the Battle for Groningen from 13–16 April. Groningen was the HQ site for the *Sicherheitsdienst* (SD), the intelligence division of the SS, in northern Holland. Although the Battle for Ortona on the west coast of the Italian peninsula has been re-called as a major urban campaign for the Canadian Army, the combat for Groningen involved substantially more Canadian soldiers and tank crewmen. Canadian artillery support was withheld for fear of injuring too many Dutch civilians. The Canadians crossed the Dutch frontier to move on to Delmenhorst, a Lower Saxony city 6 miles west of Bremen. (*NARA*)

(**Above**) British infantry of the 49th West Riding Division move cautiously through the Dutch city of Arnhem during the 'Second Battle' for that locale. The first attempt to seize Arnhem and its bridge across the *Neder Rhine* ended in defeat as a 'bridge too far' in September 1944, as Operation Market Garden drew to an unsuccessful Allied attempt to cross the Rhine. The 1945 battle for Arnhem ended on 16 April as British infantry and tanks battled house-to-house to liberate the town. (*NARA*)

(**Opposite, above**) British tankers atop an AVRE with its petard spigot mortar gun while German prisoners, with their hands on their heads, are escorted to the rear by a solitary British soldier after the 'Second Battle' of Arnhem came to a conclusion in mid-April. Many British 1st Airborne paratroopers and glidermen, who were captured in September 1944 after surrendering at Arnhem and Oosterbeek at the end of Operation Market Garden, were soon to be liberated, in part by tankers of the British 7th Armoured Division's 8th Irish Hussars, from their captivity at *Stalag* XIB at Bad Fallingbostel, a Lower Saxony German town. (*NARA*)

(**Opposite, below**) American soldiers of the 55th Armoured Infantry Battalion of the US 11th Armoured Division of Patton's Third Army move through smoke that emanated from a blazing German building in Wernberg on 22 April. The infantrymen were accompanied by an M4 medium tank of the 22nd TB with its crew-members vigilant for German snipers as enemy resistance was fanatical at times. This veteran unit, which assisted in the relief of Bastogne in December 1944, crossed the Rhine via a pontoon bridge on 29 March at Nierstein. During its drive through Bavaria, elements of this division liberated Nazi concentration camps at Mauthausen and Gusen. On 5 May, the 11th Armoured Division captured Linz in Austria prior to linking up with advancing Soviet forces. (*USAMHI*)

British and American leaders meet in the Middle East in May 1943, following the successful Operation *Torch* and defeat of Axis forces in Tunisia, to plan the invasion of Sicily. These titans of Allied victory in the west include British prime minister Winston Churchill, who is seated at the table with his trademark cigar (*centre*). The trio behind him (*from left to right*) include: RAF Air Chief Marshal Arthur Tedder; Royal Navy Admiral Andrew Cunningham, Commander of the Mediterranean Fleet; General Harold Alexander, C-in-C 18th Army Group. To the far left of Churchill were Anthony Eden, Britain's Minister for War, and General Alan Brooke, Chief of the Imperial General Staff (CIGS). Seated to the right of Churchill were Generals George C. Marshall, US Army Chief of Staff, and Dwight D. Eisenhower, Supreme Commander of Allied Forces. Standing to the far right was General Bernard L. Montgomery, C-in-C British Eighth Army, who was to achieve fame and glory as the commanding general of the Allied 21st AG in north-western Europe. This august team first forged the victory in the Western Desert at El Alamein in November 1942 and then across the entire north African littoral to north-west Africa's Atlantic coast. Then they co-ordinated the capture of Sicily in August 1943 by Patton's Seventh and Montgomery's Eighth Armies, which ultimately forced Mussolini's Italy out of the Axis partnership. These political and military leaders held together the Allied coalition that endured the protracted, rugged combat up the Italian peninsula with the US Fifth and British Eight Armies from Salerno in September 1943 to Cassino and Anzio through the first half of 1944 prior to Rome's 5 June capture, a day before the storming of the Normandy beaches. Another eleven months of gruesome Italian combat ensued at Kesselring's Gothic Line with a polyglot Allied 15th AG under Alexander (that included North Africans, Brazilians, and a Jewish Palestinian brigade) before crossing the Northern Apennines to quickly fan out across the Po River Valley in April 1945 to liberate all of northern Italy from the Nazi yoke. From the Normandy invasion to the assaults across the Rhine River, these Allied leaders continued their co-ordination of American, British, Canadian, Polish, Free French and other nations' units to liberate Western Europe and defeat the Nazis in their heartland. (*Author's Collection*)

The notable American Army and air commanders that contributed mightily to Allied victory in the ETO are shown seated at US Army 12th AG's HQ at Bad Wildungen on 11 May 1945, three days after the Nazi surrender. Seated in the front row (*left to right*) were Generals William Simpson (Ninth Army), George Patton (Third Army), Carl Spaatz (Commander, US Strategic Air Forces in Europe), Dwight Eisenhower (SHAEF Commander), Omar Bradley (12th AG), Courtney Hodges (First Army), and Leonard Gerow (Fifteenth Army). Standing (*left to right*) were Generals Ralph Stearley (Commander, IX TAC supporting First Army), Hoyt Vanderberg (Commander, IX TAF), Walter Bedell Smith (Eisenhower's ubiquitous COS), Otto Weyland (Commander, XIX TAC supporting Third Army), and Richard Nugent (Commander, XXIX TAC supporting Ninth Army). These military architects of the ever-increasing American armed forces' strength as the war progressed conducted the eleven-month campaign with their British, Canadian, French and Polish allies across north-western Europe on the ground and in the air, defeating both the *Wehrmacht* and the *Luftwaffe* in bitter combat that both liberated and devastated large swathes of the continent. The price for freedom in lives, wounds, homes, possessions and treasure, from Nazi tyranny that gripped Europe from 1 September 1939 to 8 May 1945 was indeed all too expensive, but wholly necessary to overcome the genocidal despotism that was Hitler's Third Reich. (*NARA*)

References

Allen, Peter. *One More River. The Rhine River Crossings of 1945*. Charles Scribner's Sons. New York, 1980.

Atkinson, Rick. *The Guns at Last Light. The War in Western Europe, 1944–1945*. Henry Holt. New York, 2013.

Clark, Lloyd. *Crossing the Rhine. Breaking into Nazi Germany 1944* and *1945 – The Greatest Airborne Battles in History*. Atlantic Monthly Press, New York, 2008.

Diamond, Jon. 'The Americans Have Crossed'. *WWII Quarterly*. Sovereign Media. McLean, 2014.

Elsob, Peter. 'Battle of the Reichswald'. *Ballantine's Illustrated History of World War II*. New York, 1970.

Ford, Ken. *The Rhine Crossings 1945*. Osprey Publishing. Oxford, 2007.

Ford, Ken. *The Rhineland 1945*. Osprey Publishing. Oxford, 2000.

MacDonald, Charles. *The Last Offensive*. Konecky & Konecky. New York, 1973.

Neillands, Robin. *The Battle for the Rhine*. Overlook Press. Woodstock & New York, 2005.

Whiting, Charles. *Bounce the Rhine*. Avon Books. New York, 1985.

Zaloga, Steven. *Remagen 1945*. Osprey Publishing. Oxford, 2006.

Notes

Notes